MW00605886

# Special Agent In Charge

*3/31/14*

*For my long time friends,
Pat and Gary Seale, with
warmest regards,*

*Forrest Guthrie*

Forrest G. Guthrie

*with*

*Linda Haymond-Bock*

*&*

*Lane B. Guthrie*

Published by
OnLineBinding
A Division of Knopf Enterprises

Copyright © 2014 Forrest G. Guthrie

All Rights Reserved.  No part of this book may be reproduced, stored or transmitted, in any form without the prior written permission of the author.

Printed in Jacksonville, FL, USA.

ISBN 10: 1611339413
ISBN 13: 978-1-61133-941-3

Library of Congress Control Number: 2013922747

Published by OnLineBinding.com

1817 Florida Ave
Jacksonville, FL 32206
Phone: 904.674.0621
Fax: 904.356.3373
Email: info@onlinebinding.com

**Front Cover Photo:**
From REMEBERING JACK by Tom Wolfe, Jacques Lowe, Robert F Kennedy Jr., Hugh Sidey, and Thomasina Lowe. Copyright © 2002 by permission of Bulfinch.  All rights reserved.

# Forrest G. Guthrie
*Special Agent In Charge*
*U.S. Secret Service*

When I applied for a job with the United States Secret Service, I never in my wildest imagination could envision what my career would be like.

I started my career in Birmingham, Alabama in October 1952 and transferred several times to different locales. As an agent in the Secret Service I served under and helped to protect seven different Presidents and several Vice Presidents of the United States and their families. I also protected a myriad of foreign dignitaries from around the world. When these notables from other countries arrived we were their designated protectors.

When a protectee leaves the United States to go to a foreign country, advance preparations must be made at the locations where they stay and visit. These locations have to be secured to ensure their protection and safety. Over a span of 25 years, I made many advance trips both domestic and foreign to make preperations for visits of elected officials. I also investigated and solved numerous conterfeiting and forgery cases.

I have the utmost respect for our Secret Service and have praise for all the people I have been privileged to work with.

Now, if you want to go on an adventure through my previously untold world of the Secret Service, come with me. Let me start at the beginning of my government service.

Warm wishes during the journey,

*Forrest G. Guthrie*

p.s. I have changed some names to protect privacy.

# DEDICATION

To Marilou,

For all the love, support, and care you invested in our children and me throughout the past 64 years. I couldn't have had this life, if you were not in it. - Forrest

For all your support while we talked, collected, researched, wrote and rewrote. You ensured us a harmonious place to collaborate. - Linda

# ACKNOWLEDGEMENTS

This memoir has been several years in the making and a labor of love that fulfilled a deep desire for both authors. For Forrest it was to record his life and leave it as part of his legacy to his family and to respectfully honor The Service and those who have so honorably and proudly served. For Linda it was an opportunity to fulfill her life's ambition of writing a book.

You might say it was something on both our bucket lists.

We both are abundantly thankful to our Heavenly Father for giving us life, health, and the opportunity to have come together in this endeavor. We are also thankful for the lives and experiences we have had while under your care and protection.

We will be forever grateful to:

Forrest's wife, Marilou, for her loving support, encouragement, creativity, and inspiration throughout this project. Her perspective added to our exploration. We were also the lucky beneficiaries of many wonderful home cooked meals she prepared during our work. Marilou fed our bodies, minds, and souls.

Linda's husband, Gus, for his strength, perspective, patience, and encouragement throughout this project. You sacrificed a great deal to allow us to focus on completing this common goal.

Forrest's son, Lane, for doing research, scanning and archiving photos and being a constant source of encouragement for us to complete this project.

Linda's mother, Carol, for having faith and providing constant encouragement. Without your sacrifices and support we would not have the tools we needed to make this possible.

# INTRODUCTION

*Linda Haymond-Bock*

At different times throughout our lives new people enter our world. Some stay for a short time, some remain a lifetime. Some we wish we had met years before, because our time with them will never be enough. At first meeting and often for years to come, we do not know who these people are, what they have experienced, what they will teach us, or what they might come to mean in our lives.

Ten years ago a man entered my world by chance or maybe by God's will and great design. He is a quiet, humble, kind, patient, southern gentleman with soulful eyes and a calming presence about him. When I met this man, I didn't know who he was or what he would come to mean in my life. I never imagined all the places he had ventured, the famous lives in which he was intertwined, the interesting things he had experienced or the information he stored in his mental vault.

As years passed I learned more about this man and now have the honor of calling him my friend. I have watched my friend in many different situations. Most of the time he doesn't say anything but reminds me regularly, not through words but through actions; the value of humility, the joys of friendship, the rewards of kindness, and the importance of faith.

My friend is a constant source of inspiration and encouragement to follow my dreams. One of which has always been to write a book, which he has been pushing me to do for years. What better first book than the story of the  life journey of a unique man who has touched my life and the lives of many others, in a very powerful way.

I am the recorder of this life, not the one who lived it. Through the hours my friend and I spent together gathering documents, looking at photographs and mementos, meticulously confirming details, he was talking...sharing the story of his life.

As you read this book, you will experience a life journey. I hope it will be like it was for us, a couple of friends, sitting together, talking about life's experiences. My time with my friend was so much more than just writing a book; it was sharing a world, an era, and experiences that I would not otherwise have.

In the pages that follow you will learn a great deal about my friend. There were times however, when I asked him a question and he chose not to provide an answer because of his honor and commitment to his profession. No doubt, there are other stories my friend could tell, but those are locked away in his mental vault. Those stories, no one will hear.

Now walk through a life that will unfold before you as it was told to me and lived by my friend; a life that I am fortunate to have been a part.

# Table of Contents

# From The Fields I Was Called

World War II was raging during my high school years in Albert-ville, Alabama. My senior year I received a letter from the Selective Service shortly before my 18th birthday in 1945 instructing me to report on a certain date and time to go to Ft. McClellan, Alabama. I went to the prescribed place and caught the bus. Then I spent the next three days going through my physical and processing.

Shortly after graduation I received another letter that I was drafted and was to report on July 10th. On July 13, 1945 I was sworn into the Army at Ft. McClellan. They lined us up alphabetically and every 7th man they were putting into the Navy. I didn't want to go into the Navy and as they progressed through the line I tried to figure out if I would be the seventh man...the guy in front of me was it...he was going to the Navy and I got to stay in the Army.

T. J. Carnes, a classmate of mine, was with me in the processing at Ft. McClellan. After we were processed we were marched to the train station and counted off into the box cars. The train engine was steam fired by coal and gave off cinders which came in through the windows.

We were sitting on wood benches the whole trip. The passengers all shared one other thing, "ring around the collar." That train was dirty!

We didn't know where we were going or how long we would be traveling. We were still in our civilian clothes and had box lunches to eat. We traveled all night and the next day we arrived at Camp Shelby near Hattiesburg, Mississippi.

We got off the train, got into formation and marched to a warehouse where we were given barracks bags and went down the line for each item of Army issued clothing. We were asked what size we usually wear, but it didn't really matter because sometimes we got our size and sometimes we got something bigger.

They were really careful about our shoe size and gave us a size larger because the socks were so thick. We received a package to put all our personal clothes in and send them back home. The only personal items I had left were in my pocket. The next day we were ordered to pack up all our gear and fall into formation. We sat on our barracks bags and waited, and waited. Then we marched to the station and boarded a train again to somewhere unknown.

We traveled two days and nights arriving at Camp Fannin outside Tyler, Texas. This time when we came off the train we formed into platoons and companies. One platoon was moved into one side of a barracks. In the middle was a room for the platoon sergeants, then another platoon was on the other side of the barracks.

Texas was hot! It averaged 100 degrees every day, one day it was a hot box of 106 degrees. It was miserable. I didn't have much choice about what was going on in my life, but I did make one decision the moment we went into our barracks, I was getting a top bunk. You know the reason why? I didn't want people hanging around on my bunk. I figured if I was on the top that wouldn't happen.

In the bunk below was a guy named Smith. He wasn't the sharpest tool in the shed, but he was a good guy and didn't seem to have any of the unfavorable behaviors some of the other guys had. Smith had trouble making his bed to regulation and when inspection time came he couldn't seem to get everything in the right place. I would tell Smith to do his best and then I would come in and tighten his bunk up or fix his gear for inspection. I knew that if he didn't do well it could affect me, his bunkmate, and possibly the whole platoon.

Another guy I remember was Johnson. He was an older man between 35 and 40 years old from Illinois. He just couldn't learn to march. The platoon sergeants would take him out while we were doing other things and make him march and march. He still just could not get it. So on our final inspection at the end of our 17 weeks of training, Johnson was put on latrine duty...the platoon sergeants were not taking any chances.

I hadn't seen T.J. for a while. I didn't know where he was and he didn't know where I was. About midway through the 17 week cycle, I found out that T. J. was assigned to a warehouse where they were receiving used uniforms and equipment. I don't know how he ended up with that job. We visited some after that.

We were in what was called a wartime training cycle. Part of the course called for village fighting. They used live ammunition in that exercise. It wasn't uncommon for someone to get hurt or killed, but fortunately no one in our platoon got hurt. We also had to train with flame throwers. We had demonstrations by instructors, then each of us had to take a turn with the flame thrower. We had been warned that one of the problems with this weapon was the trigger sticking.

You see a flame thrower generates tremendous heat and shoots out fluid when the trigger is pulled. The natural response when the trigger sticks is to want to throw the wand down to the ground, but that is the most dangerous thing to do because the fuel and the flame keeps shooting out.

Imagine it like a water hose on full blast that bounces around the ground. We were cautioned to hang on even if our own hand was being burned because letting go could cause a major catastrophe. The only way to stop this thing if it was out of control was to turn off a valve on the back pack and the guy working the flame thrower couldn't do it himself.

Each man in front of me took a turn with the flame thrower and I took mine with all going well. Next up was Smith, he pulled the trigger and it hung up just like we had been warned about. Smith hung on and didn't swing the wand in either direction. If he hadn't done what the instructors told him to do several of us could have been burned. Smith was commended that day for hanging on. All the times I helped him in training were repaid in that moment of time!

A few days before completing training we were told what war theatre we were going to. I was told I was going to the European Theatre. When I left training I had a two week delay to report, so I could go home and see my family. Then I was to report to Ft. Pickett, Virginia.

I took the train to Memphis and then boarded a bus to Birmingham. Trains and buses were crowded with the war going on, so there were no seats. I was a standee — stood all the way to Birmingham only sitting down at the occasional stops along the way. Then it was on a bus from Birmingham to Gadsden and finally a bus from Gadsden to Albertville.

Grandad White had a heart attack a few years earlier and he had fallen ill again while I was in training. As soon as I got to Albertville I took the one and only taxi in town to my parent's home and stored away my barracks bag. My folks, who were teachers, and my sister

Marian, were at school, so I took the taxi back to town and walked to my grandfather's home.

Grandad was in bed when I arrived and we talked for a while. Since it was getting close to time for school to close and my parents would be going home, I said to Grandad, "I am going to go home and see my parents for a while and I will be back to see you again soon." Grandad said, "You may see me, but I may not see you."

I went home to have dinner with my folks. My Aunt Jewel White came over during dinner and said grandad had passed away. He was right, he wouldn't see me again. Some said he waited for me to come home and to send me off into the world, actually into a devastated war zone. He said goodbye, I'm not sure that I ever did.

The two weeks with my family passed with such speed it was hard to believe I needed to board a train and begin my journey to the European Theatre.

First stop...Gadsden, Alabama to board a train for Chattanooga, Tennessee. From there it was on another train to Camp Picket, Virginia.

Throughout my travels I didn't see a single person from all the platoons of men I had been in training with. But I did feel slick in the new uniforms I had been issued at my current post, Camp Picket. In three or four more days we were sent on to Camp Shanks, New York, outside New York City. I learned that getting a pass to the city was no problem.

I really didn't have much to do except make muster every day and stand ready for whatever they had planned for me next. We did train on how to climb up a cargo net on the side of a ship. It wasn't a real ship, just simulated it...going to the European Theatre I thought the possibility might exist that I would need to get on or off a ship this way, but at least I wasn't in the Navy.

In between the sporadic training and musters, I decided to travel into New York City. I had never been in a city of that size or diversity, so some can't believe that I went alone. I rode the subway several times, taking different routes. I saw the scenic attractions like the Empire State Building, Times Square, Radio City and the park looking out at the Statue of Liberty.

I never went out and visited her during that time in New York, but I did take a lot in. I did it by myself because I didn't know anyone else around me well enough to know what they were going to be like in the city. Some of them seemed like they could be a little wild and I wanted to see the sights… not get into trouble.

One of the highlights of my journeys into New York City was being at Times Square for the celebration on New Year's Eve 1945/1946. It was cold, but it was really something to witness. A few days later I would leave America. But first I had to get on a ship, a Navy Liberty Ship. What happened? I thought I was in the Army.

When I boarded the ship and received my bunk assignment it was in the bottom of the ship. The bunks were stacked five or six high in a large room at the bottom of a ladder. Also near the ladder were a few empty 50 gallon barrels. I wasn't sure what those were for, but I would soon learn.

As I was settling in, a First Lieutenant came through our area asking if anyone could type, he needed a typist. I had been told not to volunteer for anything in the Army and I wasn't going to volunteer for something on a Navy ship. But he came back through again and I told him I had a year of typing in high school, but was a little rusty with the touch method.

The First Lieutenant said they wanted to do a newspaper on the ship and needed someone to type it up. Was I interested? He explained some of the privileges like an identification card that gave me front of the line privileges in the chow line. I thought it was a good opportunity, so I agreed and was issued the special pass.

It was shortly after sunset the ship pulled out into New York Harbor. The ship started moving and I was among many who were seasick before we hit open water. I realized pretty quickly that I wasn't going to be able to sit at a desk and type while looking at a piece of paper and rock back and forth. I had to tell the First Lieutenant that I couldn't be his typist.

The days ahead made for a cold, stormy January crossing. The ship tossed and rocked. There were times when we weren't allowed on deck to get fresh air because the seas were so high. The few times I did go on deck the waves often looked like walls that were going to collapse on top of us. It was horrible to be closed up in the ship...I found out what the 50 gallon drums were for because I was seasick during the entire crossing.

I thought getting a shower would make me feel better, but the showers were salt water.... a lot different than a fresh water shower. I had heard it was different, but I really needed a shower so I gave it a go. That wasn't one of my better decisions, the soap didn't wash off and I was sticky... so much for feeling better.

# The European Theatre

After seven or eight days we came into port at La Harve, France. The ship was at the far end of the dock. We formed up with all our gear and marched about a mile to the train station. Our first sight was several very nice Pullman trains. I was excited that the trains in France, and our new mode of travel, would be so comfortable. It was welcome after the ship.

"Keep marching boys" was the order...then we got a look at our train, a freight train with boxcars that were called 40 by 8's (forty men and eight horses). We didn't have horses, but we sure had 40 men per car. It was frigid; the copper electric wires outside the La Harve train station were covered with ice.

We were loaded in the cars with one small window, a sliding door, and a little coal stove with a 4" chimney made of sheet metal. There wasn't any coal or kindling in the car, no seats, and no bunks. Just a cold car, packed with men going somewhere in the European Theatre and we didn't know where or when we would get there.

This was one of many times I witnessed how resourceful people can be. Soldiers soon realized that the trains ran on coal and there was spillage along the tracks especially around stations, so when we stopped they began to gather up all the coal they could find.

They were resourceful but it didn't necessarily mean we were warm. It took a lot to get a fire going to a temperature to burn the coal and there just never seemed to be enough coal. Oh well, we tried and it kept us occupied and it taught us to work as a team. To this day when I think about that trip I remember vividly that my barracks bag was just about empty because I had on every article of clothing I had in an attempt to stay warm.

We traveled a few hours before the train stopped around 10 pm and there along the railway was a mess kitchen set up to serve us. I had not eaten much while on the ship and we hadn't received any food since we left the ship. Here in the middle of who knows where in France, was hot food and an opportunity to get off the train. I'm not sure how many other Americans came through that place with no name that we stopped at in the middle of the night, but for me it is a place I will never forget.

We rode that train for two or three days that way...hours on the train, then all of a sudden we would stop and there was a mess kitchen.

We arrived at Marburg, Germany which was designated a replacement depot. It was an abandoned German base and war barracks with windows and doors, for the first time in a long time I was able to get warm. A bath house was located about a mile away from my barracks.

I gathered up my hygiene gear, bundled up and made the walk to the bathhouse where I joined the long line of men waiting for the luxury of a brief shower. After waiting for hours, a trickle of men moved into the bath house. Then a Sergeant arrived and said the water heaters were broken and there would be no more showers today, try again tomorrow.

When tomorrow came we were required to turn in our new uniforms they had issued us back in the states in exchange for used uniforms. So I found out how the Army got new uniforms shipped to Germany from the U.S.A. We wore them over. We didn't have to give up our boots or undergarments, just the uniform items. Then it was time to get on another train.

This was an actual passenger train, much more comfortable than our previous railway experiences. I still hadn't found anyone I knew from training. It seemed odd because there were a lot of us, but who knows where all those guys went. This trip was two or three days and our next stop was Bremerhaven, Germany, a former German Navy compound and port.

My new home was an old German Navy barracks with a parade ground right next door. Thank goodness Johnson wasn't here, he wouldn't have wanted to see that big area to march on.

We were formed up and marched to chow, but to our surprise we were told to find our own way back once we had eaten our fill. The sergeant's instructions were to return to our barracks and remain there.

For some this was a bore because they didn't have anything to do, but I always carried something in my pocket to read and that's what I did to pass the time. That night a sergeant came in and announced that we would be assigned to units the next day and should have our barracks bags packed.

In the morning, three or four hundred troops assembled on the parade ground. A group of six by six trucks pulled in and backed up to the edge of the parade ground. A sergeant with a bullhorn was in the back of one of the trucks. He started calling names and assembling those called at the back of a truck. After calling 15 or 20 names, he would tell those men the unit to which they were assigned. The men would load on the truck and the truck would leave. This procedure went on for several hours. I looked around and saw all the empty places until only three or four of us remained in the large field . The sergeant called us together and said, "You men are assigned to the 388th Military Police Battalion," and pointed to the building where we were to report. I ended up back in the barracks in the same room where I had spent the night before.  I was ready to go somewhere and didn't!

It was later that day that a First Sergeant came into our barracks and said he was looking for a typist. If anyone could fill the billet he wanted a volunteer. I didn't speak up at the time but after thinking what if I got stuck standing in the middle of a road somewhere directing traffic in this freezing cold weather, typing in an office, sounded pretty good. Later when he came through again asking if anyone could type, I decided to volunteer. So I went out and found the First Sergeant in the hallway and asked him if he still needed a typist. I told him I could type, not fast, but accurate. "Report next door to the orderly room," was all he said.

When I reported the First Sergeant sat me down at a desk in front of a German typewriter. Well, I'm thinking 'not fast' just became, even slower and accurate, and that's questionable. I asked what he wanted me to type and he pulled a copy of Reader's Digest out of his back pocket, flipped it open to a page and propped it up next to me, "Type that." I typed until he told me to stop, then gave him the page and the Reader's Digest. "You're the one I want, be here at O-eight-hundred tomorrow".

That was the beginning of my billet as a clerk for the 388th Military Police Battalion. I was a new private but everyone around me were sergeants and above. So everybody out ranked me and could tell me what to do.

I guess I did a good job because I kept getting new tasks, assignments, responsibilities and authority. Within 30 days I was a private first class, in another 30 days I was a corporal, and guess how long it was before I was a sergeant...30 days.

It took me a little longer to make staff sergeant, six weeks. It just so happened that I fell into that organization at a good time to be promoted. Many of the soldiers who had fought through the war years were going home and I was a replacement.

I had a desk and a small area to prepare the daily pilferage report. You see the Army was spread all around the port and the town so we had supplies and ammunition all over the place. Almost every night people would take things, so each day all the supplies were inventoried at each site. I would combine all the reports that came in from the individual sites into one pilferage report.

During this time our commander was Colonel D. L. Dutton. He was regular Army and was the Bremen Enclave Provost Marshall. All the MP's in the areas in and around Bremerhaven to Bremen were under his command. I heard scuttlebutt that Colonel Dutton's First Sergeant was getting ready to rotate home and it wasn't too long after that I got a call to report to the Colonel's office.

When I reported, a Captain, who I believe was the Colonel's aide, asked me if I was interested in coming to work for Colonel Dutton in the First Sergeant's place. I didn't have to think about it, I knew that not only the MP's were under Colonel Dutton's supervision, but so was CID (Criminal Investigative Division) and I would get to be involved with a lot more than military police activities. I was in!

After a few months I got called back into the Colonel's office because he wanted to talk to me about going to OCS (Officer Candidates

School). That was the second time I was offered an opportunity to join the officer ranks, did I tell you about the first time?

It was during basic training. We were out in the hot Texas sun doing some kind of training when a jeep rolled up with a young lieutenant in it. He talked to one of the sergeant s who was training us. The Sergeant called out, "Guthrie, you are to report to the orderly room." When I got there our company commander, a Captain, was at the desk. I didn't think this was going to be good. What had I done or what had happened back home?

The Captain eased my mind right away (well as much as a boot at attention can be at ease). He said, "Guthrie, the Army needs junior officers to lead in this war. We see from your file that your IQ is good and you are doing well in your training, so how about becoming an officer. You can go right now to OCS and once you complete it all you have to do is agree to extend your service one year beyond the original commitment."

Hmmmmm.....now that one I had to think about. Well maybe not, my first gut reaction was no, but I asked to think about it overnight. The next day I was given a pass to come back and give the company commander my decision.

My answer, "Sir, I thank you and the Army for this fine opportunity, but my parents want me to finish up my time in the Army and get back home and start college just as soon as I can. It's something we have been working and planning for. So I feel I must decline your offer to go to OCS." I was worried he might think I wasn't a good soldier, but he said he understood and that he wished me well in the Army and what lay ahead.

So anyway, here I am in Colonel Dutton's office, standing in front of his desk and I get the pitch... "Guthrie, the 3rd Army needs more junior officers to continue our work here in the European Theatre. You've done a good job here and I believe you will make an excellent officer. All you need is three references from field grade officers, which is no problem, because I will be one and I have two Majors who will do the same, complete OCS and in 90 days you will be a Second Lieutenant." Here comes the Oh by the way... "All it takes is you agree to extend in the European Theatre for one year beyond your current commitment."

I needed a little bit of time to think about it so I asked the Colonel if I could think about it overnight. The next day I returned to the Colonel's office and gave him the same response I did back in boot camp the first time OCS was offered.

Even though I turned it down, I felt really good about being offered OCS by two different commands. The Colonel didn't have a problem with my decision, as I spent the rest of my time working for the command.

Then I got notice that it was time for me to rotate back to the states. I was relieved of my duties and was secured to the base while waiting for our ship home to arrive. About a week before we departed Bremerhaven a request came down for me to escort a prisoner (Army soldier) back to Munich. My travel restrictions were lifted so I could make the trip.

I agreed and was provided with six sets of original travel orders and another soldier who was to assist me with the transfer. For the next two days and nights we traveled by train to Munich. I didn't sleep much because the guy who was supposed to help me... well he didn't.

When we arrived in Munich I delivered the prisoner to the military jail and got a delivery receipt. With my mission accomplished and still a few days before the ship sailed I decided to take in the sights.

I went to Vienna, Austria, and saw the Vienna Boys Choir when they performed at a military recreation facility. I visited the Bavarian Alps and saw some really beautiful country.

This was a really bad time for the German people. There was so much destruction and devastation throughout their country but the German people I interacted with during my travels were friendly.

Then it was back to Bremerhaven to board the ship and sail to New York...that was how I ended my summer in 1946, seeing Germany, and saying goodbye to the European Theatre.

The ship I came back to the United States on had formerly been a cruise ship. As a staff non-commissioned officer I was assigned to officer quarters. The accommodations were much better than on the liberty ship that had taken me to France. It sure beat the racks stacked five high and 50 gallon drums.

From New York I traveled by train to Ft. Bragg, North Carolina for out-processing. I was given my original discharge papers in triplicate and a small Wallet size copy. I rode the bus from Ft. Bragg to Atlanta, changed to another bus in Gadsden and the final transfer was to Albertville.

My date of honorable discharge from the United States Army is November, 1946.

# It's Over, Over There

When I got discharged and went back home my folks wanted me to go right to college, but I wasn't ready to jump right into that.

My mom's brother, Doyle White, lived in Atlanta and was college educated but he was making a living buying and selling used cars. With his advice, I started buying cars and selling them. I'd go to car auctions and buy a car for $500 or $1,000 and sell it for $1,200 or $1,500.

Uncle Doyle and I had tow bars for our cars that had a vacuum brake set-up for the car we were towing. All I had to do was push a lever on the steering column that put the brakes on the towed car before I pressed the brakes on my car, so we had brakes on both cars and we were much safer.

We went from Atlanta to New York by train to buy cars in 1948. I bought a new 1948 Ford and a 1939 Ford while we were there. It was a long ride back and I only got about $900 for the 1939, but I was driving a new car.

After about a year in the "car business" my parents told me my sister wanted to go to college in Birmingham at Howard College. They had decided to move to Birmingham, rent a house, and get teaching jobs. They thought I should come too and get started on my college education.

That year I enrolled as a full time student at Birmingham Southern. The tuition was high but what made it possible for me to go there was my GI education assistance and I worked at TCI (Tennessee Coal Iron and Railroad Company) Fairfield plant. My starting pay was $1.21 per hour and ending it was $1.29.

The plant smelted ore and made iron. My job was in the tin mill. During this process, the steel was pressed and rolled into coils of tin. The sides were then trimmed which caused  scrap. I would fill out the weight tickets with the amount of scrap that was measured after the trimming of each coil so there was a true weight calculation for the finished coil.

# My Marilou

I attended a church near my home, but one night a friend wanted to go to another church for a program. During the program I looked across the room and saw Marilou Shubert. She was pretty and had a smile on her face. We had friends in common so I asked to be introduced and ended up giving her a ride home that evening.

I didn't know how old she was, but had been told she was a senior in high school, so she had to be 17 or 18 right? Marilou's family had a phone, so I called to make arrangements to take her out to a recreation area along with some friends to swim and have a picnic.

While we were all talking that afternoon something came up about age, each person told how old they were and then when it came time for Marilou to tell her age somehow the subject got changed. It wasn't until a few days later someone told me her age...15!!! That wasn't going to work so I decided I couldn't make any more dates with her... she was too young. That wasn't the end of the story though. It was the beginning of a relationship and marriage that has lasted more than 64 years.

Marilou left her makeup pouch in the glove compartment of my car, a 1939 Ford (by accident, she still to this day professes). I decided it would be the right thing for me to return it to her. So I drove to her house and that was my undoing. From the beginning her parents were supportive of our dating, even with the age difference.

Marilou graduated from high school at the age of 16. She wanted to learn business machines, so she attended courses at a school downtown for three or four months. When she graduated she couldn't get a job because she was only 16. She applied to TCI and got turned down because of her age.

That didn't deter Marilou though, she went back again later and saw the same man and asked him for a job again running business machines. He said he would hire her as a mimeograph operator until she turned 17 and if she had done a good job until then, she could apply to operate business machines.

Marilou turned 17 and got promoted. On her 17th birthday I put a ring on her finger and on January 6, 1950 we were married at her parent's home.

The government had been paying me $75.00 a month and paying my tuition. The first year we were married I started getting $105.00 per month and Marilou was making $250.00 a month. I was driving an old 1942 Ford that I had bought from Army surplus, reworked, put a new grill, bumpers and a new paint job on it so it looked like a 1947.

We were living on a little over $300.00 a month renting a bedroom and kitchen on the second floor of a house owned by the Birmingham Assistant Chief of Police, E. H. Brown. In 1951 I transferred to Auburn, so we moved to Marilou's parent's home.

I would get up early each Monday morning and drive about 120 miles to Auburn to be there in time for my first class. Then I would stay at my grandparent's house Monday through Thursday nights and drive a truck for my uncle picking up fertilizer in Tuskegee when I wasn't in class or studying.

Friday afternoon after class I would drive back to Birmingham to spend the weekend with my Marilou. That was my routine for a year until I graduated with a Bachelor of Science in Business Administration on May 30, 1952.

# What's Next?

After graduation Marilou and I went with her parents, Claude and Joy Shubert, to St. Petersburg Beach, Florida for a vacation week. Before I go into much detail let me digress about my father-in-law for a moment:

> Claude B. Shubert lived in Jasper, Alabama and during the depression, he was finally able to secure a job as a substitute postal employee. He worked himself up to the position of Postal Inspector, assigned in Atlanta, Georgia. President Franklin D. Roosevelt visited Warm Springs, Georgia from time to time and Mr. Shubert was assigned to be the Presidents' mail carrier between Warm Springs and The White House.
>
> Mr. Shubert would drive to Warm Springs to receive The White House mail, which he carried in a leather padlocked bag, handcuffed to his wrist, and return to Atlanta to spend the night. The next morning he would fly to Washington, D.C. to deliver the mail to The White House and to receive any mail going to President Roosevelt in Warm Springs. Mr. Shubert saw the President from time to time and when he saw him on April 12, 1945 he returned to Atlanta and told Mrs. Shubert, *"that man is not long for this world."* The president died on April 12, 1945.

During our trip to St. Petersburg, my father-in-law asked me what I was going to do next. I told him I wasn't sure and he said to me "*Next to the Postal Inspection Service, I like the Secret Service, so when you get back to Birmingham I suggest you put on your suit and go see the local Agent In Charge.*" In those days the Postal Inspectors worked closely with the Secret Service.

So that is what I did when I got back. I put on my suit and went to the **Birmingham Secret Service Field Office located on the third floor of the Federal Court House.** I just walked in cold and introduced myself to the clerk behind the counter, Mr. James B. Phillips.

I told Mr. Phillips that I had just graduated from college and wanted to apply to be a Secret Service Agent. He called over Special Agent In Charge (SAIC) Terrance Ryan, whom I introduced myself to and asked him what I needed to do to apply for the Secret Service. Mr. Ryan said the Secret Service had an inspection process where **inspectors come from Washington to evaluate offices and it was my** lucky day because one of the inspectors, Mr. Michael Torina, (who was originally from Birmingham) just happened to be there.

Mr. Torina talked with me for a long time asking me a lot of questions about my background, my education, military service, etc. He said, "We always have a need for new agents. In fact right now we need someone for the White House garage that knows engines and how to work on them."

I thought I might be getting in over my head because I didn't know anything about Cadillac engines, but I didn't say anything. Mr. Torina had applications with him and said I would need to fill one out to start the process. Then if I got the temporary appointment I would have to take the Civil Service exam in the future. Mr. Torina instructed me to fill out the application that night and bring it back the next day along with my wife.

The next day Marilou and I returned to the field office with the completed application. Mr. Torina and Mr. Ryan took the application along with Marilou into an office and closed the door.

They were in there a long time. She said later that among the many things they talked about was the fact that from time to time in the Secret Service, agents were required to relocate and they wanted to know if she would have a problem with that. Marilou told them, "I can fry the bacon anywhere my husband can make it."

That must have been the answer they were looking for because when they came out Mr. Torino said he was going to take my paperwork to Washington. If everything in my application was good to go, Mr. Ryan would contact me and administer a Civil Service exam in the Birmingham office then send it to Washington to be graded.

A week later I received a call from Mr. Ryan asking me to report to his office to take the Civil Service exam. It was in three parts. The first part had two photographs, one was a street scene and one was an office scene. I could look at each picture for about five minutes, then I had to answer about 20 questions about the first picture.

Next was another section of the test completely unrelated to the pictures. Finally the last part of the test was related to what I saw in the second picture. When I completed the exam Mr. Ryan packed up the test and the answers and shipped it off to Washington to be graded.

A few weeks later I received another call from Mr. Ryan. "Guthrie, this is Ryan, you sure as hell are causing me a lot of trouble. You passed the damn Civil Service exam and now I have to spend a bunch of my time doing a damned full field investigation on you. You know this might take six weeks or more to get everything completed, so I'll call you when I have more information." And he hung up.

That was one of my first experiences with Mr. Ryan's colorful vocabulary and candid approach. It wouldn't be the last. In the meantime I had to make a living, so I applied for a job at Hayes Aircraft as a parts chaser. The company was refurbishing C-130's. I would go to all the areas where parts were stored trying to find the parts they needed for the refurbishing on different aircraft. If I could not find the parts needed and there were multiple aircraft that needed the same item, they would have to manufacture some parts.

Three months later I got a call from Mr. Ryan, I had been accepted and was to report to the Birmingham Field Office to begin my career as a  Secret Service Agent!

# Appointment to The Service

My first day on the job as a Secret Service Agent was October 6, 1952. At that time the Birmingham Field Office consisted of a clerical office, Mr. Ryan's office, and another office that had two or maybe three desks in it. The two agents shared that tiny office. For investigative purposes, we covered the state of Alabama with a staff that consisted of the SAIC, Terrance Ryan; SA Darrell Marsh; the clerk, Mr. James Phillips; and me, the new kid.

My first assignment...type up my own appointment papers and then Mr. Ryan took me upstairs to be sworn in by Federal Judge Seybourn Lynn. After that, Mr. Ryan called an Alcohol, Tobacco, Tax Unit Agent named O'Day to take me out somewhere and let me practice shooting a pistol to see if I might qualify to carry a firearm. Mr. Ryan let him have the pistol that had been shipped to Birmingham for my use when I qualified with it.

Mr. O'Day took me out to the edge of town, to a very thinly populated area. It's in Homewood, Alabama today. O'Day put a target up on a tree and showed me how to fire a pistol. Well, of course, I knew about firearms having been in the military and one thing and another, but I had never fired a pistol before, however I knew what a sight picture was.

I practiced with a pistol under O'Day's instruction and then he said, "Okay, we're going to go for the record now." I fired the pistol under Agent O'Days direction and qualified. He seemed to think that was pretty good that a fellow could qualify the first time he tried.

On the way back to the office, O'Day told me that he was about to retire in the next week or two. He was retiring from the ATU after some 30 or 35 years of service. He seemed to be a super nice guy, conscientious, and well qualified for what he was doing.

When we got back to the office he told Mr. Ryan that I had qualified with the pistol and Mr. Ryan seemed pleased about that. He issued me the pistol, but of course, I didn't have any credentials. So Mr. Ryan wrote a letter and Mr. Phillips typed it up.

The letter read "To Whom It May Concern. This letter introduces Special Agent Forrest Guthrie of the U.S. Secret Service who is authorized to carry firearms and who is authorized to perform the duties of a Special Agent of the United States Secret Service."

Mr. Ryan signed the letter and I was to carry it inside my coat pocket at all times in case someone questioned my authority to carry a pistol. I carried that letter for two or three months until my official credentials were sent from Washington. I never had to show the letter, but I had it just in case.

Most of my training outside of the office was with Joe Roberson, a Postal Inspector Investigative Aide. He would tell me what we could and couldn't do with regard to interviewing suspects, and he pretty much knew what the Secret Service wanted and he for sure knew what the Postal Service wanted. We got along pretty well. Joe had been doing that work for a number of years, and as a matter of fact, sometime later on, Joe Roberson's son became a Secret Service agent.

In those days, agents never had the luxury of having another agent go out with them on a case. I don't remember ever working with another agent or going out of the office with another agent to work on a case for several years. We did a lot of work with the Postal Inspector's Office and sometimes you could get one of them to go with you on check theft cases if you felt you might have an arrest.

My first day on the job working outside the office I went with Joe Roberson on some check cases he had in the works. Our building was next to a town square by the Birmingham Police Department. Joe wanted to go in to talk with the detectives about a check case and while we were waiting I looked at a board where they had pictures of 20 or 30 people who were wanted for crimes but had evaded capture.

After Joe and I finished our business we headed to a little diner on the square for some lunch and took a seat on stools at the counter. While we were sitting there I looked over at a guy sitting along the other side of the counter and thought he looked familiar. I kept looking at him trying to figure out where I had seen him before.

Suddenly, it hit me, I just saw his picture on the detectives most wanted board!! I told Joe we needed to step outside and when we did I told him what I had seen. I asked him to go get the police while I stayed there and watched the suspect. Joe brought the police over with the man's picture from the board in the detective's office and it was him. They arrested the guy on the spot. From then on we were very welcome in the detective's office and they were always ready to help us with information.

I learned a lot from Joe Roberson and Mr. Ryan. Mr. Ryan told me early on and many times while I was working for him "Forrest, whenever you're working, ALWAYS have your gun on your person. Never leave your gun anywhere else." Whenever I was going out of the office, Mr. Ryan would always yell out to me, "Forrest, do you have your gun?" My answer was always, "Yes, Mr. Ryan."

Mr. Ryan had been a policeman before he became a Secret Service agent. He had been in two or three shooting scrapes as a policeman, and he said to me one afternoon while we were talking, "Forrest, always remember one thing. If you get into the kind of situation that requires it and you know you're right, shoot first." He said, "It'll be a lot better for you to be on the stand defending yourself than it would be to have that guy, a criminal or suspect or whoever it is, on the stand defending himself for killing you."

Mr. Ryan was cautious about the use of a weapon and that sort of thing, but he said, "If it's really questionable and you're being threatened, don't hesitate to shoot the first shot. You don't necessarily have to be shot at in order to respond." I always remembered that and I still do.

About two weeks after I started with the Service I received notice that I was to report in 30 days to the Oklahoma Field Office in Oklahoma City.

Seems that was the plan all along and I guess that is why they asked Marilou how she felt about relocating. I only spent a total of six weeks in Birmingham before Marilou and I packed everything we owned in our car, a 1950 Chevrolet (except a few items that we shipped in a cedar chest by rail) and headed to Oklahoma City.

I reported for duty the first week of December, 1952. This was Marilou's first of many opportunities to fry bacon in a new place.

At that time, the Special Agent in Charge of the Oklahoma City Field office was Tom Hanson. There was one other agent in the office named Bill Gilliam. The clerical employee was a fellow named Geron Brown. I continued my training under Mr. Hanson. They all had some years of experience and were very helpful to me. It was still a situation of working alone and we didn't have radios.

I called the office on a pay phone every two hours to see if I was needed anywhere. I was at a real disadvantage in Oklahoma City because I didn't know a soul in the area unlike Birmingham where I knew people who knew people. That was part of how you got information and found people, you had to know people.

I didn't let that hold me back though. I got to know the area and worked on getting to know people. Among the people I met and became friends with was Assistant U.S. Attorney, Billy Potter and his wife, Patty. I understand that Billy went on to later become the United States Attorney.

I made my first arrest (alone), soon after I got to Oklahoma City. I don't remember who it was and I don't remember what case it was, but I was out one afternoon at a rooming house taking handwriting specimens to see if I could find out who forged a check. I obtained specimens from this person and I examined his writing. There was a definite match. So I asked him to come outside and sit in the car, and as soon as we got in the car he confessed.

A week or two after I arrived in Oklahoma City, with a total of maybe two months of service, here I come walking in to the office with this handcuffed guy that forged a check. It seemed like I was off to a good start in my career!

One thing all agents were required to do was read books from a designated list. I had a year to complete the list. I would read one of the books and then do a short report summarizing the book and send it to Headquarters. I usually made a summary about a page in length. I never had one rejected, so I guess they were okay.

I don't recall all the titles of the books that I had to read, but one of them was Money and Banking. They thought we ought to know a good bit about how a bank works. Other than what the Agent in Charge and older agents were telling me about duties and reading the books, that was all the training I had during my first year. I don't know how many cases I closed but it was quite a few.

# Special Assignment

At that time, President Truman was in office and President-elect Eisenhower was taking office on January 20, 1953. About the first part of January we received an office memorandum. There was hardly any telephone usage in those days, between Headquarters and the Field Office, unless it was some type of an emergency. Everything was done by memorandum and the ones that Headquarters used were blue. We called them *"blue blazers"*.

A *blue blazer* sent me to Denver (in January of 1953), to, for want of a better word, "baby-sit" The Doud House at 750 Lafayette Street. This was the home of President Elect Eisenhower's in-laws. They had gone on a trip. Of course, I assumed that the Doud's were going to Washington to participate in the inauguration.

It was a large two-story house. It had a basement in it and President Eisenhower had a lot of his war mementos, photographs, objects and memorabilia that he had collected as a General.

My duty was to sit in the house from 7 p.m. to 7 a.m. I had the midnight shift so to speak. When I got to Denver, Inspector E. A. Wildy was there, he had been sent out there to get us started.

The Agent in Charge was a fellow named Earl Schoel. There was an agent there named Lane Bertram and one there by the name of Bob Grube. They had another agent that was going to help in the Doud House, but he didn't come until 2 or 3 days later and his name was Mike Mandulay.

Of course, this was January in Colorado, so there was a lot of snow. We had to keep the house warm or everything would freeze. One of the things that I had to do was throw a little coal in the furnace once in a while and make sure that there was enough water in the system. I could tell how high the water was by looking at a sight glass.

So here I was, on my first "protection" detail, house sitting. I was to sit up in the house from 7 at night until 7 in the morning, but in the daytime they didn't have anybody there. I guess they thought the neighbors would watch it in the daytime.

After Mike Mandulay got there, we shared those duties for about three weeks. That was my first time at the Doud House, but unbeknownst to me it wouldn't be my last. I went back to Oklahoma City and resumed my duties in the Field Office. I was doing the same things that I had been doing before and continued my training.

# Last In, First Out

During President Eisenhower's campaign one of the promises he made for when he got into office was to reduce the number of Federal employees. The process is called 'Reduction in Force' or 'Riff'. I'm here to tell you, he kept his promise. Along about April of 1953, a "blue blazer" came and it turned out that since I was one of the last employees hired, I was going to be riffed on June 30th.

In the memorandum, there was a possibility of employment with what at that time was called the Narcotics Division. They had a few vacancies and Secret Service Chief U. E. Baughman put in a note that maybe if I would apply with them they would take me on as a Narcotics Agent.

By that time I had seen two or three Narcotics Agents and heard about what they did, and I didn't think that was what I really wanted to do. Just prior to this time, SAIC Hanson had been promoted and sent to San Francisco, and he had been replaced by an Agent in Charge named Paul M. Hart from Houston.

When the memorandum came I talked to Mr. Hart about it. He said "Well, maybe it won't come to pass. Maybe they'll work something out between now and June 30th. But in the meantime, it might be a good thing for you to write a memorandum to Headquarters and tell them how much you like being an agent and if they hire in the future you would definitely want to come back."

So I wrote the memorandum, sent it off, and prayed every day that word would come back that I could stay in the service. June 30th came and there had been no news. Marilou was seven months pregnant at the time with our first child, Lane. We had no insurance, and now I had no job.

But I had faith we would be alright. I had money in the bank and we were going back to Birmingham.

At 3:00 p.m. on June 30th Marilou came to the office with the car loaded with all our possessions (except the trunk we had crated up again and sent by rail). I had turned in my weapon, credentials, case files, and all my other equipment, so I was ready to go. Marilou remained in the car.

I thought Mr. Hart might let me leave then so we could start out for Birmingham. But he wouldn't let me leave until 5:00pm. You know, I really believe he thought there was a possibility that he might get a phone call telling him I didn't have to leave. The call never came. So we drove part way to Birmingham that day, and the next day we were back home. I didn't do anything for a while, you might say I took a little vacation. I did call some friends to let them know we were back and to make some job inquiries.

About a month after we got back to Birmingham, a letter came in the mail via Special Delivery wanting to know if I was interested in further employment with the Secret Service. If so, would I report to Washington, D.C. at my own expense for reappointment. Washington was a high cost area even back then in relation to the rest of the country, but I thought, well, this is the opportunity I've been praying for, so I'll do that.

I wrote a letter that said I would be happy to be reappointed and would report at my own expense.

In the meantime; what I didn't know was that an agent who had been employed in the Birmingham office while I was in Oklahoma City was leaving.

I received a telephone call from Mr. Ryan advising me I would be reappointed to the Birmingham Field Office on September 1, 1953. My prayers were answered. Lane was born in August and I started as a Special Agent on the designated date, September 1st. So I worked in Birmingham for another year and a half on a variety of check, counterfeit coin, and bond cases.

I was on the road a lot...traveling the entire state of Alabama. Back in those days the per diem rate was $9 a day. You could get a nice hotel or motel room for about $3 a day, and if it had an air conditioner in the window you could get one for $4 a day, but that was a luxury I couldn't afford. With Mr. Ryan, I didn't get to choose where I stayed when I made a road trip because Mr. Ryan would tell me exactly where that was going to be. If I was going to Montgomery to work, he'd say "Guthrie, you stay at this particular hotel. They know me in there. You'll get a good room and I'll know where you are. If I have to call or send you a telegram, you will get it there."

I was never called on the phone unless it was a dire emergency. It was always a telegram. If I was going to work Montgomery for a week, when I got through with my cases and knew what day I would be returning to Birmingham, I had to send a telegram to the office so they could look at it and say "Guthrie's about to leave Montgomery." If they needed me for something particular, they'd send me another telegram or call me on the phone and leave a message at the hotel.

From October 4-31, 1953, I was assigned to the Washington Field Office and the White House Detail, for familiarization purposes, and for them to determine if I was a suitable candidate to be assigned to the White House Detail  permanently. I was present with the detail for President Eisenhower's first birthday in the White House. He celebrated in Hershey, Pennsylvania on October 14, 1953.

On October 18, 1953, I went with the White House group to Laredo, Texas where President Eisenhower met the Mexican President and they dedicated Falcon Dam near McAllen, Texas. It was during this trip that I worked the follow-up car for the first time and took my first flight in an airplane. The Service was broadening my horizons!!

The Service, at that time, employed about 250 agents and whenever an agent was in Washington on a temporary assignment, the standard procedure was to call Chief Baughman's secretary and ask for an appointment. It was the first time I saw him. Of course, I was pretty nervous, but he was a nice fellow and put me at ease.

While I was there he said, "You will be due for promotion from GS-7 to GS-8 on such and such a day. I've been working trying to get a change made to promote new agents from GS-7 directly to GS-9." He said, "If you're willing to let this date slip a little bit I might be able to promote you directly to GS-9." I told him, "Well, I'm perfectly willing to do whatever is agreeable with you."

Sure enough, I went back to Birmingham, and a month or two later I was promoted to Grade GS-9. I may have been the first or one of the first agents that went directly from GS-7 to GS-9.

In March of 1954 I received a memorandum transferring me to the White House detail at Fort Benning, Georgia. There was a small detail there protecting the Eisenhower grandchildren. Another memo came not too long after cancelling the transfer.

Then almost two years after joining the service I received a memorandum on July 15, 1954 sending me to my first formal training. I was to report to Washington, D.C. in September for 30 days at the Treasury Law Enforcement Training School. We had Secret Service, Internal Revenue, Customs, and Alcohol Tobacco Firearms Agents all in the classes.

We were taught how to make arrests and how to conduct searches of people and property. We also went into an indoor range to qualify with our issued weapon, a 38 Colt with a 4-inch barrel.

# Washington, D.C. Field Office

In December of 1953, I was sent on a 30-day temporary assignment to the Washington Field Office located in the main Treasury Building. The 30-day temp assignment for new agents were primarily to have supervisors in the Washington Field Office look us over to see if they think we're suitable for assignment to the White House. During the assignment, they had me working personnel cases, which was a type of case I'd never seen before. I had a rather interesting case during the assignment. It was a Protective Research Subject (PRS) case.

An elderly woman was brought to the office by a White House Police Officer. I have no memory of what her name was, but she was a street person and she was wearing a big, heavy overcoat. She had been to the White House, and had wanted to see the 'death birds' that were kept there. When the lady was brought in, I was assigned the duties of talking to her and finding out what her problem was. She was talking to me about the 'death birds' that were kept at the White House, and if they weren't at the White House, they had to be in the Treasury Building. She wanted those birds! I couldn't shake her away from this, and I was unsure what to do with her.

At that time, Mr. Tom Kelly was the Assistant Agent in Charge at the office and he was the one that supervised the agents. I went to him and told him about her problem, and he said, call the DC Police Department and ask them to send over a female officer because we are going to have to commit her to St. Elizabeth's Hospital for mental evaluation. I got all the information from her that I could before the female DC police officer arrived. Then we transported her to St. Elizabeth's in a van. When we arrived, the female officer said, "You'd probably better stay here in this office because we've got to take her around here in this room and search her." They were gone a long time, it must have been almost two hours she was in there and all this time I'm wondering what's going on.

It turns out that this old lady had money stashed all in her clothes. She had it pinned and sewed everywhere that you could imagine that anybody could put dollar bills, 5, 10, 20 dollar bills on their person. It took, more than two hours for them to find all of her money, unroll it or unfold it, then count it.

This lady had on her person some two or three thousand dollars. I guess it was her way of safeguarding what she had, but it was still strange. I do not know what happened to her and I never figured out what the 'death birds' were. Strange.

They evidently thought I was suitable for assignment to the White House Detail, so in November, 1954, I received a transfer to the Washington Field Office on a permanent basis, and we moved up there. Marilou would be frying bacon in another place.

This time we had a little bit more than would fit into our car and instead of just the two of us, our son Lane was with us. As when we went to Oklahoma City, we didn't know the area and we didn't know anyone. We found a motel on Highway 1 in Alexandria, Virginia to settle into temporarily until we could find a suitable home or apartment. After the first night in the motel we knew this wasn't going to work for long because we didn't have a kitchen. I had to go off to work and when I came home the next day my wife and baby were gone. I asked the desk clerk if he knew where they were and he said they were in an apartment at the back of the motel.

My wife might have been a young girl from the country but she knew how to get things done. This was just one of many examples over the years of Marilou's tenacity and ability to make a home for us, no matter where we were.

It wasn't too long before we moved into the Fairlington Apartments in Arlington, and Marilou was driving around the city like she had lived there all her life. Being the wife of a Secret Service Agent wasn't always an easy job, especially for one whose husband was on the White House Detail. We worked a lot of hours and we didn't make a lot of money. My Marilou always made the most with what we had and I always looked forward to coming home.

I was doing different types of cases at the Washington Field Office. One of the very first cases that I remember was a new challenge. I had never worked a counterfeit case probably because there wasn't that much paper money counterfeiting at that time. I'd worked a counterfeit coin case or two. Of course coins seemed to be more valuable at that time.

We had a counterfeit case that involved two men and a woman. They had been traveling through several states passing counterfeit $20 bills and they were fairly successful with it. They had changed cars two or three times, but basically they had used the same names or variations of these same names at the motels where they were staying. So late one afternoon, we got the idea that they were in the Washington, D.C. area. Tom Kelly, the acting SAIC, called all the agents in (we now had radios in all the cars).

We had a meeting about it and it was decided that agents would pair up. We knew what kinds of accommodations these people had been staying in before they got to Washington. We got out the phone directory and divided up all these possible places that we thought we ought to go and check and see if we could find anybody registered under any of these names or variations of these names.

There was an agent named Howard Munson and he and I were a team. We had our list of motels/ hotels to go to and the third or fourth place we went, the suspects were registered. So we back out and call the office and say "We've got these names registered tonight at this particular hotel." The other agents were called in and Assistant Special Agent in Charge (ASAIC) Kelly, began making different assignments.

We sent a bellboy up to see if they were in their room and they were. We went up and knocked on the door. They had two connecting rooms and the people were undressed. The men had on boxer shorts and the woman was wearing a thin little nightgown. We had found out during the investigation that these three had been traveling together for some time and that the woman had been staying with one fellow one night and the next night she'd stay with the other one. This was a woman who had a college degree and was really a nice looking person.

We needed to search the room and their belongings. So you know what my job was in that counterfeit search? My job was to keep an eye on the woman. "Don't let the woman out of your sight," was what I was told by the SAIC.

You see there had been a couple of previous cases in which women had stashed counterfeit notes in body cavities. The SAIC didn't want me to let this woman out of my sight in case she had something stashed and tried to dispose of some evidence. So my job was to watch her, and I did.

Counterfeit notes were found in the room and we got ready to take the people away. The woman wanted to get out of the nightgown and put some street clothes on. She asked me to look away. I said, "I'm sorry. You heard what the man told me. I've got to watch everything you do." She said, "Okay."

Off came her night gown and she changed into street clothes right there. I don't remember what happened to the case, but I'll never forget my assignment. My first counterfeit case and the assignment that I had was to watch this attractive woman. I sure got a lot of kidding about it later.

While assigned to the Washington Field Office I started working to supplement the White House detail going where the President was going while in town. They used to call these 'movements'. I was doing quite a bit of that really.

There were a lot of times the President went on official functions around Washington, D.C. If it was a black tie function, we agents would need to be dressed appropriately. I did not own a tux at the time, so I rented one from a store that several of us agents used. At one of these functions I sat across from John L. Lewis, a prominent union leader. He was very cordial, but what really struck me was his bushy eyebrows!

# President Eisenhower Detail

From April of 1955 to August 1957 I was permanently assigned to the White House, so it was just a matter of moving across the street from my current office.

President Eisenhower went somewhere the night of the last day I was assigned at the Washington Field Office. It seems to me like I had some sort of a patrol in a car, it was with Special Agent Johnny Grimes. The President stayed out late and he didn't go back home until 1:00 or 2:00 in the morning.

My assignment with the Field Office was over at midnight, but in reality, of course, that didn't matter. So Johnny and I went ahead and did what we had to do until we were relieved. At any rate, due to the hour, I drove the Field Office car home and got in about 3:00 am. I didn't have to get up and go to work in the morning at 8:30 or 9:00 because I was going to the White House the next afternoon and I thought, well, I'll just drive the Field Office car in when I go to the White House at 3:00 pm.

Later that morning I get a call saying "Where's the car?" I'm not even out of bed yet, but I had to get up and take the car in. It really didn't bother me because I knew they needed it, but I didn't think anybody would call me for it because they knew I'd bring it when I came.

When I got down there and I was joking with Mr. Kelly about it, how he had kept me over two hours overtime on my last day at the Washington Field Office and everything. Of course, he was kidding when he said "Let me tell you, Guthrie, I want you to know that your commission is good 24 hours a day and it says U.S. Secret Service, not Washington Field Office, or White House Detail." He said, "You're commission is good anytime, anywhere and you probably want to keep that in mind in the future." Of course he was laughing the whole time.

During my years with President Eisenhower we made multiple trips. He worked hard but he also liked to have time away from Washington and politics to enjoy his three passions; golf, fishing and painting.

I made a lot of trips outside the country with President Eisenhower. One time we went through Iceland to Switzerland. We went to Canada, Mexico, Bermuda and a number of other places. It's difficult to get them in sequence because after I left the White House, many times when he was making a foreign trip, I was called back to make advances. The purpose of an advance was to survey places the President would be going, eating, or staying; arrival and departure points, and roadways he would he traveling. The agent's job was to work with the local authorities and police departments to ensure we had adequate security, personnel and addressed any potential concerns prior to the President's arrival. We also had to make arrangements for the President's car, a backup and follow up cars for his Secret Service detail.

On one occasion, in 1960, I was called back to do advances in South America for a trip that he was taking. I helped with an advance in Montevideo, Uruguay. Then we went to Buenos Aires, for a short time, but I spent most of the time in Montevideo on that trip. Another time, I was given a temporary assignment with the White House Detail when President Eisenhower made a trip to Manila in the Philippines and then to Taipei which was Free China and to Seoul, Korea.

By this time the President had a new jet used as Air Force 1 on that trip. I was assigned to the 12:00 pm to 8:00 am shift and was assigned to fly in the back-up plane, which was an identical jet having the same interior features as Air Force 1. If Air Force 1 should have any problems on the trip the back-up plane would be substituted, and we would then stay with the crippled plane until it could be repaired and we would then re-join the Presidential party. It was a long trip but fortunately everything went smoothly with Air Force 1. At the end of that trip, we returned to Hawaii and stayed several days.

# What a Great Country We Live In

In June 1955 President Eisenhower took a driving trip through New England. The weather was beautiful and he was traveling in an open convertible driven by his agent driver. The other agents and I were in a convertible follow-up car. There had been some publicity about the trip so when we drove through small towns and even in sparsely populated areas, there were many people lined up to see the President. They would stand on the sidewalks of the towns, families would be gathered at the end of a road, or sometimes it was just one person standing in the middle of nowhere...all were waving their hands or flags and clapping when we drove by.

During that trip and even today I struggle to describe the overwhelming feeling of pride, admiration and respect that was generated in me when I saw the response of American citizens all along our route. For a person like me, it was a privilege to witness and to be a small part of it.

The trip lasted for several days providing President Eisenhower many opportunities to enjoy his favorite passions: golfing, fishing, and painting. Fishing in the area was said to be exceptional, and the scenery offered numerous creative scenes for Ike to capture. A lot of people probably do not know that President Eisenhower painted.

Actually, over the years Marilou and I received several Christmas cards from President and Mrs. Eisenhower that were copies of his paintings.

The Service had two identical 1938 Cadillac convertible sedans used as follow-up cars. At that time there were several cars, Lincolns and Cadillacs, available for use by the president and first lady. All the cars were manufactured with input from the Service on safety and security features. The follow-up cars we selected for this trip were 1938 Cadillacs that had been sent back to the factory to be remanu-factured. They had 500 HP engines, could keep up with anything and could outrun almost everything. Both follow up cars and President Eisenhower's car were driven by special agents trained in driving. Agent Dick Flohr was a favorite driver of the President. Actually word was that Flohr had for a time driven then General Eisenhower during World War ll.

During the trip the President stayed with friends and all of the agents stayed in a nearby hotel or motel when we were not on duty. One exception was the couple of nights we spent in a lumber camp. This camp was really isolated with a set up I can best describe as Army like barracks for the workers to reside in and there was a building set up as a chow hall. The workers weren't there because the camp was inactive that time of year.

A large lake was nearby and the scenery was really beautiful. It was kind of like we agents were on a vacation too because we were out of DC and got to enjoy some gorgeous areas of this country that this Alabama boy had never seen.

# President Eisenhower's Trip to Geneva

On July 15, 1955 we departed Washington, D.C. en route to Geneva, Switzerland, for the meeting of the Big Four, the United States, England, France and Russia. I was traveling in the press plane. When we reached Geneva, I would be on the midnight shift. En route we had a four hour refueling stop in Keflavik, Iceland. While on the ground we had at least three kinds of weather, *all cold*. It rained, it snowed, it sleeted, and turned back to rain again.

We were traveling in a brand new American Airlines Super Constellation which was fully loaded, so much so that food and drinks were stacked along one side of the aisle. On take off from Washington the plane was slow leaving the runway. It took longer than usual to get to a flying altitude and the tail was dragging. I was concerned because I wondered what would happen if we needed to land and the tail was dragging...not a good scenario.

Later on I had a chance to ask the Co-Pilot about it and he said that since the plane was new and had not been flown a long distance before, it had been loaded incorrectly. They had to burn a certain amount of fuel before the plane could be completely leveled. It took two or three hours to do this.

Interesting!!!

One of my friends and a mentor was Special Agent Emory Roberts. We arrived in Geneva at 7:55pm and were scheduled to work the midnight shift. Our hotel was the Hotel Du Rhone located in the middle of town on the Rhone river, which was contained by concrete walls, and streets were on each side of the river, an interesting place. Emory and I decided we would be tourists until 1:00 or 2:00pm each day. Then we would sleep and get ready for our midnight shift again.

We learned that each day a ferry crossed Lake Geneva to France and returned to Geneva after a period of time. One morning Emory and I took the ferry to France, and of course they had an immigration and customs office there. When they saw our Diplomatic Passports, it was absolutely no problem to walk around the small French town, then return to the ferry. When we returned the officials did not need to see our passports again. It was an informative and interesting trip.

At the conclusion of the trip, each of us received a machine autographed photo from President Eisenhower and then Secretary of State John Foster Dulles in appreciation for our service during that trip.

# Headline: President Has Heart Attack

On August 14, 1955 we traveled in Air Force 1, the Columbine II with the President to Denver, Colorado where he stayed at the Doud's house, 750 Lafayette Street. On September 19, 1955, we traveled up to Fraser, Colorado where the President fished until September 23rd, then he returned to Denver[1]. On September 24, the President played golf, then during the night he became ill and after being seen by his doctor, it was determined he was having a heart attack. He was trasnferred to Fitzsimmons Army Hospital[2]. The transfer took place in the Presidents car, so as not to draw public attention and concern by calling an ambulance.

A heart specialist, Dr. Paul Dudley White, was brought in from Boston. We stayed in Denver about six weeks while the President recuperated. In those days there wasn't a lot that could be done for a heart attack. They didn't have bypasses or stints or the procedures they do today. All they could really do was have him rest and hope for a good recovery. For the next several weeks when I went on shift I worked at the Doud House or the hospital[3].

---

1    The President's Appointments, Dwight D. Eisenhower, Friday, September 23rd, 1955.

2    The President's Appointments, Dwight D. Eisenhower, Friday, September 23rd, 1955.

3    The President's Appointments, Dwight D. Eisenhower, Friday, September 23rd, 1955.

One day our SAIC, Mr. Jim Rowley came to me and said that the Columbine (Air Force One) was going back to Washington, D.C. for maintenance and offered me the chance to fly back to spend a few days with my family. I jumped at the chance. On October 11th, I boarded the Columbine and flew to Washington. As far as I know, I was the only passenger. What an experience!!

On October 21st, I received a call telling me the Columbine was ready to return to Colorado that night. I boarded the aircraft and was told we needed to go to Boston first to pick up Dr. White, then we would proceed to Denver. We didn't leave Washington, D.C. until about 11:00 pm but Dr. White was waiting for us when we arrived in Boston and boarded immediately.

Shortly after we were airborne a steward came and told us they were preparing two bunks for us so we could sleep during the flight. They had, I think, other bunks in that airplane. Dr. White had the lower bunk and I had the one up top. The Columbine was probably the world's safest plane. It was the only propeller plane that I know of where all four engines could be started at the same time for quick departure.

The Air Force personnel on the aircraft were very considerate and helpful during the flight. I couldn't have asked for better accommodations. Then and to this day I think to myself: *"Can you imagine, me, a person from rural Alabama, getting to fly on the best aircraft in the world?"*

We stayed in Denver, while the President recuperated. On November 11, 1955, we flew back to Washington, D.C. and stayed two days at the White House. On November 15, 1955 we went by car to Gettysburg, arriving at 1:00 pm. Evidently the event had been well publicized as we found a large number of vocal, friendly people assembled along the streets and at the city center. There, a platform

was used by President Eisenhower to make appropriate remarks re-
garding the warmth of his reception. The crowd also serenaded First
Lady Mamie Eisenhower with Happy Birthday. Then it was on to the
farm.

We stayed at Gettysburg until November 22, 1955, when we went to
Camp David for an overnight visit, then back to Gettysburg. We finally returned to Washington, D.C. with the President on December
10, 1955.

.

# Working the Crowds in a Black Tie

President Eisenhower went to Panama from July 21 to 23, 1956 to attend meetings with the leaders of Central American and South American countries. What stands out about this trip, to me, were the tremendous crowds of friendly, pressing people calling out the President's name. It seemed they just wanted to get close enough perhaps to touch him.

I was working the follow-up car, which means it was my job to walk beside the President's car. It was a hot day and all the agents were wearing suits and white shirts with black ties (the ties were issued to us). The motorcades of the other leaders were ahead of us.

People in the crowd near us were being pushed by people behind and every step we took we had to push people away. People got between the cars and then had to walk with the cars. Somehow one agent got two or three feet away from the car and could not get back. We finally inched and pushed our way through to the unloading area which had been kept relatively clear of people.

We were all overheated and exhausted and our clothes and socks were wringing wet with perspiration. Then we discovered that our "issued" black ties had bled so that we now not only had black ties on, we had large black ties on our white shirts!!! It ruined my shirt. That trip taught me a lot of lessons about just how quickly a situation can change. It was a foreign country. They did not understand us and we did not understand them. I sure was glad everyone in the crowds were friendly, but their zeal for President Eisenhower created a stressful situation for us. This incident also brought to light the need to have extraction methods for those types of crowd situations.

# The U. S. S. Canberra

President Eisenhower, was to attend a meeting of other leaders in Bermuda. He went from Washington to Norfolk, Virginia on March 14, 1957, and boarded the U.S.S. Canberra, a guided missile cruiser, for a leisurely cruise to Bermuda. We went down to the Bahamas and stood off Cat and Eleuthra Islands. We just floated around with the engines idling while everyone enjoyed the ship, the sun, and the scenery. The accommodations were good and the food was excellent.

One afternoon the Captain's Gig, a small boat, was lowered into the water so President Eisenhower could go closer to the island and ride around it. They also placed another smaller boat in the water for us (the agents) to use as a "follow—up" boat and I was chosen to ride in this boat. What an experience. As we got closer to shore the water became clearer and clearer, so that at thirty-five or forty feet down you could plainly see the bottom and several different kinds of fish of various sizes. Some were said to be barracuda. The island appeared to be uninhabited, at least where we were. One day the Navy put on a demonstration of the guided missiles, which was extremely interesting to us. From the mainland they sent a drone aircraft to fly at an altitude of a mile or two from the Canberra. The plane was visible with the naked eye. The Canberra fired a missile to intercept and shoot down the drone.

The interesting thing is that about three fourths of a mile away the missile's first stage fell off and was tumbling through the air, visible with the naked eye. In the meantime the Navy wanting to be sure they got the drone, fired a second missile. This missile went up, homed in on the tumbling tube from the first missile and exploded. Then the first missile went on, hit the drone and exploded. What a demonstration of the homing ability of the missiles

After the demonstration, we arrived in Bermuda at 2:20 pm on March 20, 1957. President Eisenhower attended the conferences and on March 24, 1957 we departed Bermuda via a U. S. Air Force plane to Washington, D. C. arriving at 11:15 am.

# The Special Little Things

Over the years, President and Mrs. Eisenhower did special little things that made me feel that they cared about their agents and their families. You know what they say, *it's the little things that make a big difference.*

Our daughter, Karen, was born in January, 1957 at Alexandria General Hospital, and mother and daughter came home a few days later.

One morning Marilou received a telephone call from the White House inquiring if she expected to be home that afternoon as Mrs. Eisenhower wanted to send her a package. The White House used easily recognized black Mercuries mostly driven by uniformed drivers. That afternoon one of those cars parked on the street in front of our apartment and the driver brought a package to the door. When Marilou opened the door, the driver presented the package saying, "Compliments of Mrs. Mamie Eisenhower." Marilou thanked him and the driver departed.

When Marilou opened the package it contained long stemmed "American Beauty" roses, and the card said "Best wishes, Mamie Eisenhower." Both Marilou and I always felt that was thoughtful and a most appreciated gesture by the First Lady. The delivery by the White

House car surely enhanced our standing in the neighborhood!!

On May 24, 1957, I received notice that I would be transferred back to Birmingham effective August 12, 1957. So on July 17, 1957 I wrote a memo to SAIC Rowley requesting an autographed photo of President Eisenhower.

Within a few days I received from Mr. Rowley a photograph from the President which he personally inscribed as follows: "*For Forrest G. Guthrie with appreciation of loyal and efficient service at the White House, and with best wishes*," Dwight D. Eisenhower (See page 81). At the same time I also received an autographed photo of Mrs. Eisenhower which she personally inscribed as follows: "*To Forrest G. Guthrie with my best wishes*," Mamie Doud Eisenhower.

During the time Mr. and Mrs. David Eisenhower lived in Atlantic Beach, Florida for about two years beginning in July 1971, Mrs. Mamie Eisenhower visited them. After her departure, I received another autographed photograph which is signed, "*For Mr. Forrest Guthrie, a family friend*," Mamie Doud Eisenhower.

The third autographed photograph was received directly from Mrs. Eisenhower in Ocala, Florida, shortly before my retirement in 1977. It happened like this: Mrs. Eisenhower was taking a vacation by car and she had spent a few days at the Augusta National Golf Course, then motored down to Clearwater, Florida where she stayed a few days with her sister. On the way back to Gettysburg, she wished to stay overnight in Ocala, Florida, have dinner with some friends an continue her trip the next day.

I went to Ocala to assist with the advance. Mrs. Eisenhower stayed at a motel just off the interstate. When her car stopped at the motel curb, she got out, took my arm and allowed me to show her to her room. Later she met her friends at the restaurant for dinner.

We were using the room next to hers as a command post and it had an interconnecting door. The next morning Mrs. Eisenhower opened the door and inquired if I was there, and when I responded, she invited me into her room. She had finished her packing but one suitcase was still open and I saw four different poses of photographs there. She said "Mr. Guthrie, I know I have given you previous autographed photographs but l would like to give you another one. Could you choose one of these?"

So I chose one of her with President Eisenhower. Then she said "How do you spell your wife's name?" So I spelled it "M-A-R-I-L-O-U". While Mrs. Eisenhower was signing the photograph, she told me about various members of the family that I would remember... how they were and what they were doing. She went on to tell me that she had enjoyed seeing the people she had visited during her trip and that because of her age she may not make a trip like this again. She then thanked me for all the small things I had done over the years for her, Ike, and their family members.

Mrs. Eisenhower handed me the autographed photograph that said, *"For Marilou and Forest Guthrie with warm wishes."* Mamie Doud Eisenhower (See page 104). Then she took my arm and I escorted her to the car. We said good bye for the last time because Mamie died on November 1, 1979. Of all the First Ladies I had as protectees, Mamie Eisenhower was special because of the span of 20 years I had served her and President Eisenhower. Every time we interacted she was considerate, personable, courteous, and an elegant lady.

# Tactical Helicopter Demonstration

In 1960, when I was selected to go on the advance for President Eisenhower's trip to South America I flew into Washington, D.C. from Birmingham. Due to airline schedules I arrived hours in advance of the time I was supposed to report for my travel orders. I decided to kill a little time by going to the White House Detail Office. While talking to SAIC Jim Rowley, Special Agent Vincent Mroz came in.

We talked for a short time when he said, "Guthrie, since you are here and have some time on your hands, I would sure appreciate it if you would come out for a tactical helicopter demonstration at Quantico. This could be important for you to see", and so I was off.

As we drove to Quantico, Vince explained that what we were going to experience was a simulation of an extraction of the President or dignitary from a vehicle using a helicopter. In the event the President's car got pinned in or something created the need to make an extraction, this was one of the methods that were being considered. I thought, "This sounds interesting."

As it was explained to me, there would be a person in the backseat of a car simulating the president with a driver and a helicopter crewman in the front seat. They would he traveling at about 15 miles per hour when along would come a helicopter with a horse collar dangling from a cable that would scoop up the "President" and carry him away to safety. The demonstration was to be done on an unused airport runway.

The President's staff and the Service weren't sure this would be a good method of extraction. So to better explore if this method should be adopted, the demonstration would be filmed for later review.

We arrived at Quantico and here sits a car without a top similar to the one available for the President's use. There is a driver behind the wheel, but no one in the backseat. I'm thinking, I guess the guy who is simulating the President isn't here yet.

I stepped out into the winter chill with the wind blowing in my face to find out, the guy who is going to sit in the back seat just arrived... it's me. Next is a demonstration of how to get into the horse collar, and a meeting with the helicopter crew. Before I know it I am sitting in the backseat of the President's car going down the runway and in flies this big helicopter. It hovers 30 to 40 feet above the car going about 15 miles per hour and drops a horse collar, which the helicopter crewman helped me get into. The helicopter starts going up, I'm going up and there isn't any going back. As soon as my feet cleared the car, the helicopter took off going up to maybe 500 feet and going normal speed with me in my suit and trench coat dangling from a horse collar underneath. Just imagine this aircraft weighing ten or twelve thousand pounds with the fierce wind being generated by the blades, and me dangling underneath while it flies away. I finished being drawn up and was helped into the chopper about the time it reached altitude. It was cold and let's just say this was the least preferred method of travel I ever used before that little trip or since. But what a view!!

Then we flew back to the point where we started and landed. We were talking about the event when the cameraman came up and said his camera failed and he was not satisfied. He wanted us to do it again, so we did. You know, surprisingly, that extraction method was never adopted and written into our procedures. I heard later that the President and others didn't feel it was a dignified way for a President to travel.

Or maybe when the President saw the film of the demonstration, he saw the look of concern in my eyes and decided he didn't want to share in that experience. I don't blame him!

# Far East Visit

In June of 1960 , I was called from the Birmingham office to travel with the White House Detail on a trip to the Far East with President Eisenhower. Several stops were planned and the White House Detail would he stretched thin. I reported to SAIC James Rowley at the White House on June 10, 1960, and was assigned to travel aboard the backup plane, a new jet aircraft said to be identical to the plane used as Air Force One. I was assigned to the midnight shift.

We flew to Anchorage, Alaska on June 12, 1960 arriving at 10:45pm. It was my first experience with the twilight nights there. It was bedtime, but it was still daylight outside...how strange that was!

The next morning we left Anchorage at 7:15 am in clear weather, and our pilot flew near Mt. McKinley so we could see it and the nearby mountains. From the air it was really beautiful, but on the ground it looked frigid.

We crossed the International Date Line and arrived at Clark Air Force Base in the Philippines. We were off loaded to a smaller plane and arrived in Manila at 6:00 pm. En route we were flying over rice paddies and what appeared to be salt gathering ponds, scenery we were not accustomed to seeing.

The President stayed at Malacanang Palace, the home of Philippine President, Carlos F. Garcia. The President left Manila on a U. S. Navy ship to view naval maneuvers and then went on to Taipei, Formosa.

Those left behind departed Manila aboard a small plane to Clark A.F.B., transferred to Pan American Airlines arriving in Taipai, Formosa at 1:35 pm on June 17. On the Pan AM flight the hostess offered us some "Try it" items...fried bees and grasshoppers. I had never seen anything like it before!!

We stayed at the Grand Hotel, said to be owned by Chang Kai Scheck. The hotel was modern and "up-to-date", with pretty Chinese architecture and built on the side of a hill. Chang Kai Scheck entertained President Eisenhower and the official party, including me, with a fourteen course meal at noon the next day in a ball room at the Grand Hotel. The room was decorated with elegant Chinese pictures, drawings, and statues. The tables were set with magnificent plates and dinnerware. It was a good thing for me that they offered us a choice of silverware or chopsticks, as l could not use chopsticks. Each course arrived in a small portion, each in a separate clean dish, and when the course was finished the empty dishes were collected and the next course was served. I did not know what I was eating much of the time and the tastes were strange, but I ate it all so as not to offend our host. Overall, it was an excellent meal and I am unlikely to have another one like it. I am pleased to have had the experience.

While in Taipei, we had some time off and Special Agent Ed Tucker and I hailed a rickshaw and took a tour of downtown and the waterfront. The city was relatively clean and the people were industrious and very active. Ed and I did not much like riding in the two wheeled rickshaw cab being pulled by a man. We gave him a hefty tip when we got hack to the hotel, and decided to leave that method of transportation to others.

We reached Seoul on June 19, 1960. Since we were on the midnight shift we were given a chauffeured car to our hotel downtown. We left well ahead of the Presidential party and traveled the same streets to be used by the motorcade.

The streets were very wide and there were tremendous crowds of people. We were later told that when the motorcade got there, the people, all friendly, crowded in against the President's car and the follow-up car, being pushed by people 100 feet away with such force that the cars were seriously dented. It seems, again, people just wanted to get close to the President, perhaps to touch him.

This was the trip where the President was expected to visit Japan, but at the last minute some diplomatic hitch developed. The visit was cancelled. We overflew Japan.

We departed Seoul, Korea on June 20, 1960 at 6:40pm. I was on the back-up jet en route to Honolulu, Hawaii. We crossed the International Date Line and arrived at 12:45pm at Kaneohe Marine Corps Air Station. The President rested from his trip and played golf.

One day the Commanding General of the base loaned us his aircraft and his crew took five or six of us agents on an aerial tour of the islands. We flew at a low altitude to see the lush scenery then landed on the main island of Hawaii. There we were met by military cars and taken to a military base for lunch. After lunch the cars took us to see the volcano and we acted like tourists, walking as close to the volcano as they allowed. I had heard of volcanoes all my life and never expected to see one, yet there was an active volcano right in front of me. Amazing!!!

When we left the volcano, the cars took us to several places of interest, then back to our plane. We flew another scenic route back to Kaneohe. That was a really memorable day!

On June 25, 1960, the vacation was over and we left Honolulu at 5:15 pm, again I was on the back-up plane. We arrived in Washington, D.C. on June 26, 1960, at 9:00 am. I was released from the White House Detail and at 6:00 pm that night. I left Washington and returned to Birmingham at 7:20 pm.

All in all, considering everything, most of the travel was in a luxury plane, with luxurious accommodations. We were well received in the countries we visited, and the scenery was unique. This was my most favorite foreign trip while with The Service.

# The Press

There were always reporters around, but not like it is today. The White House Press Corps used to be a lot smaller than it is now. Generally speaking, it was mostly the same press people.

I don't know the exact number that traveled permanently with the President, maybe 30 or 40, because usually whenever the President traveled, we'd have a press plane. The President would travel in his plane with a few agents, and the press pool. The remaining agents and the press would share what they called the "press plane." Of course, the Service had to pick up tabs for the agents that were on there, and the press people paid for their part of the charter.

We got to know the regulars pretty well. Most of them you could rely on and others you had to be rather careful about. As a matter-of-fact, at the White House there was one guy that used to come there and he would just sit in the lobby. He would take a seat out there in one of the chairs to see who was coming and going.

If you didn't know who he was, somebody might say something that he could overhear and, of course, he would start asking questions or write something about what he heard. So we always had to be careful about that. Generally speaking, the majority of the press were good.

# President Elect Kennedy Detail

In November 1960, I had about eight years of service as an agent. I had served at the White House for about two and a half years. I was selected for the Kennedy President Elect Detail. On about November 5, 1960 I met the other agents in Boston and reported to the detail leader, Inspector Burrill Peterson. I was assigned to drive the car that was to be used by the President elect (if Senator Kennedy won). The car was a new four door Lincoln, fully equipped, white in color. I made sure the car was fully serviced and that all equipment was working.

At that time, by law, the Service only protected the President Elect and the Vice President Elect after they were elected. The Republican candidate, Vice President Nixon, already had a protective detail. But the Democratic candidate, Senator Jack Kennedy, went through his campaign with no regular protection except for protection furnished by local police departments in places where he traveled.

On election day we drove over to Hyannis Port and took rooms in a motel. After dinner, Inspector Peterson, ASAIC Behn, SA Robert Lapham, and I went to Mr. Peterson's room and turned on the TV. The election returns were showing VP Nixon ahead, and in the next hour Senator Kennedy would be ahead, and vice versa. We stayed up all night and could not tell if we had a job the next day or not. At 7:00 am the phone rang. It was Chief Baughman talking to Mr. Peterson. He was saying that the people that project these things had predicted that Senator Kennedy was going to be the President Elect and that we should go ahead and assume his protection.

By the time we got people together, it was probably about 8:30 am when we arrived at the Kennedy Compound, three waterfront houses side by side. We found that the Hyannis Port Police had been securing the place for several days. The police told us that with the race results uncertain, all the Kennedys went to bed in the center house about 4:00 am. They were apparently still asleep, so we did not bother them. An advance survey had been made and we knew where the posts were. They had picked out a place for me to park the car behind the houses. I drove the car around to the back and parked. The houses' front was on a large bay and I could see the Coast Guard boat patrolling. I could not see anyone else. As far as I know everyone else stayed in front, as a crowd was gathering.

At about 9:00 am I was standing by the car when I heard a door open on the center house, and it was Senator Kennedy. He saw me about the same time that I saw him and started in my direction. As I was the stranger in his back yard, I went to meet him, introduced myself, told him I was with the Secret Service and we had been requested to begin his protection as he was the projected winner. He seemed very pleased with that. He said he had not yet heard that projection, and his family was still asleep in the house he was leaving. He woke up first and not wanting to disturb them by turning on a television there, he was going to the house near where we were standing, so he could see how the election was going on the kitchen TV and to make a pot of coffee.

I congratulated him, wished him well, and said I was happy to be the first to do that, as well as to be the first to call him Mr. President

Elect. He said, "Please do not call me that. I am a Senator and Senator will be just fine."

He expressed an interest in the car and asked if it was mine. I told him the car was obtained by the Service for his use and we were hoping he would be willing to use this vehicle and that I had been assigned to be his driver. He walked over to the car, opened the driver's door and commented about how pretty it was and said he liked the white color. He smiled when I said, "we know". He talked with me several minutes, asking about the Service, where I was from, was I married, did we have children, and how long would I be assigned to him? I told him I expected to be with him throughout the inauguration. He was very personable.

When the Senator said he was going in the house to see about the current election results, I told him that I knew the man in charge of our group would like to talk with him for a few minutes at his convenience. He said, "Fine, just tell your man I will be in the kitchen of this house. Tell him not to knock, just walk in and I will be looking for him."

As soon as he went in and closed the door, I went between the houses and summoned Mr. Peterson and Mr. Behn and told them my conversation with the Senator and which house he was in. They went in and had their conversation with him.

The election results did not show Senator Kennedy winning until around noon. I understand he did not claim victory until after he received a telephone call from Vice President Nixon. After that, arrangements were made for Senator Kennedy to hold a press conference in the National Guard Armory.

When it was time to leave, I drove the car around to the front of the houses. When Senator Kennedy came out, his brother, Robert Kennedy, was with him. Motorcycle policemen led us to the Armory, and when the event was over we drove back to the Kennedy Compound. It was the only time I ever saw Robert Kennedy in person. If you watch the video of the arrival (it's on YouTube) I am driving the limo although glare on the windshield prevents me from being seen.

We stayed in Hyannis Port for two or three days then flew down to West Palm Beach. I think Senator Kennedy went on a chartered plane.

Aside from named supervisors, other agents are ranked by seniority on their shift. The White House had multiple man shifts at the time so that as work assignments came along it was usually the senior agent who got the job.

So with Senator Kennedy the normal expectation was that he would be met by Mr. Peterson or by his deputy, Mr. Behn, who were at the front of the house, where a crowd was gathering. Instead Senator Kennedy came through the rear door where I was. That is how I came to be the first person he saw that day, tell him he was the projected winner, and congratulate him.

What a high honor and a privilege. I have a great indebtedness to the U.S. Secret Service for letting me be placed in such a position.

*Conjecture:* I think when Senator Kennedy got up and wanted to go next door to turn on the television he looked out front and saw the crowd. Not wanting to face that group of people without knowing where the election stood he departed by the back door. How fortunate for me!!

For: Forrest G. Guthrie

*With appreciation of loyal and efficient service at*
*The White House, and with best wishes.*

*Dwight D. Eisenhower*

*To Forrest Guthrie*
*With Best Wishes-*
   *John F Kennedy*

*To Forrest G. Guthrie*

*With Best Wishes,*
*Lyndon Johnson*

Note: President Johnson signed this photo on the sleeve of his left arm(bottom right of photo) and it is hard to read.

*To Forrest Guthrie*
*With appreciation and best wishes,*

*Richard Nixon*

Photo note: personalized photo of President Nixon and Agent Guthrie shaking hands.

## *To Forrest Guthrie*
### *With appreciation and best wishes,*

### *Richard Nixon*

To Forrest G. Guthrie
With best wishes,

*Gerald R. Ford* (signature)

**To Forrest G. Guthrie**
**With best wishes,**
**Gerald R. Ford**

*To Forrest Guthrie*

## To Forrest Guthrie

### Jimmy Carter

*To Forrest Guthrie*
*Best Wishes*
*Ronald Reagan*

**Bathtub**

Was originally in the Palace that stands behind me

200.0

U. S. Secret Service

SAIC Downing, Birmingham                                    June 14, 1961

Chief

Commendation - Special Agent Forrest G. Guthrie

I have been informed of the excellent work performed
by Special Agent Guthrie in effecting advance arrangements
in Manila and Karachi and carrying out other protective
responsibilities incident to the recent round-the-world
trip by the Vice President of the United States. The work
entailed meticulous planning and long hours and frequently
called for on-the-spot judgments and evaluations. In this
the efforts by this Special Agent were fully in keeping
with the high standards and traditions of the Service.

For such fine work, which contributed to best security
and an overall smooth operation, I extend to Special Agent
Guthrie my thanks and commendation.

Chief

*Original to
SA Guthrie -
copy to field
personnel file
of SA Guthrie.
BD*

U. S. SECRET SERVICE
RECEIVED
JUN 1 6
Birmingham, Ala.

# Commendation from Chief Baughman

# Gifts from Carlos Garcia
## *President of the Phillippines*

Plaque commemorating
the Phillippines visit

Box of (Excellent!) Cigars

**Alexander's Well**

**The Doud House
Home of President Eisenhower's In-Laws
Denver, Colorado**

Commemerative plate
from Ike's first Birthday in The White House

**Forrest G. Guthrie**
*Special Agent In Charge(SAIC)*
*Secret Service*

**Forrest holding Jill**
**Standing Left to Right**
**Kent, Karen, Brenda, Lane**

Forrest and Linda at a Kiwanis meeting

**Gardens near Government Guest House in Agra, India
Near Mrs. Kennedy's residence**

**Special Agent Guthrie in Bermuda**

Ox operated water wheel for irrigation

Special Agent Guthrie
New Dehli, India 1963

## Taj Mahal

Digging in Taxila, Pakistan

**Road Project in India**
**notice the lack of any mechanization**

**Stainless Steel Pillar
Dates from Approximately 1500 A.D.**

Possibly the first known example of
stainless steel in the world.

**The U.S.S. Canberra**
**Baltimore Class Cruiser**
**Entered service in 1943**

# Aboard The U.S.S. Canberra

**President Eisenhower**

**ATSAIC Campion**
**SA Guthrie**
**SA Knight, later Director**

*For Marilou and Forrest Guthrie with warm regards*
*Mamie Doud Eisenhower*

**Forrest G. Guthrie**

**President Eisenhower Detail**

**Forrest and Marilou Guthrie**

Easter, 1963
From left:
Kent, Brenda, Karen, Jill, Marilou, Lane

**Marilou Guthrie**

# White House Christmas Card
## Last Christmas before Kennedy's Assasination

*The White House — Winter 1962*

**The White House — Winter 1962**

*John F Kennedy*                    *Jacqueline   Kennedy*

# Deer Hunt at West Ranch

A few days after we arrived at Palm Beach, Florida, we learned that Vice President Elect Lyndon Johnson had invited Senator Kennedy to visit him on his ranch near Johnson City, Texas. The nearby small town of Johnson City, Texas was named after Johnson's father's cousin, James Polk Johnson, whose forebears had moved west from Georgia[1]. On November 16, 1960 Senator Kennedy along with other agents and I went to the Palm Beach airport and boarded a new chartered jet for a flight to Bergstrom Air Force Base.

At Bergstrom we loaded into separate smaller planes to make the 75 mile flight to LBJ's ranch. I was assigned with several other agents to fly in LBJ's personal twin engine plane; piloted by two men wearing cowboy hats.

We arrived at the ranch on an airstrip located not far from the main ranch house, and as I recall, we walked with our luggage over to an outbuilding near a small ranch house, which we were using as an office. By this time a regular White House driver had been assigned to Senator Kennedy and I was assigned to the midnight shift headed by Special Agent Robert Lapham.

---

1     Wikipedia, Lyndon B. Johnson Biography

It was mid-afternoon so the midnight shift had some time between when we got settled and when our shift began. We borrowed a car from the ranch and drove several miles to a place we could get something to eat. Then it was back to the ranch house to sleep until time to get ready for our shift starting at 11:30 pm.

At the main ranch house, Mrs. Johnson left her kitchen open with snacks, coffee, and cola drinks available for us during the night. The weather was chilly and it rained a lot through the night and into the early morning. About 5:15 am it was my turn to take a little break in the kitchen and I was there drinking coffee when an inner door opened and down the stairs came Mrs. Lady Bird Johnson.

Mrs. Johnson was gracious and friendly. We exchanged "Good mornings" and a few other pleasantries before she told me she got up early to make breakfast for those "two boys" as they were going deer hunting as soon as they ate[2]. It still makes me chuckle to this day, Mrs. Johnson referring to the soon to be President and Vice President of the United States as those "two boys".

I thanked Mrs. Johnson for the hospitality and allowing us to use her kitchen during the night.  I then excused myself and headed to my next post outside.

I had not heard anything about the deer hunt, so I found SA Lapham and he knew nothing about the hunt either. He went to find Inspector Peterson and ASAIC Jerry Behn. They were in a house somewhere nearby to let them know about the hunt. We also needed to get the day shift up and ready to relieve early so they could go on the deer hunt instead of us. We'd already been up all night and had flown the previous day.

As luck would have it, it turned out that the day shift was in a house

2      Senator Lyndon B. Johnson Daily Diary, Thursday, November 17, 1960

several miles away and they were unable to get back to the main ranch house to relieve us early. You see in 1960 there were no cell phones, some people didn't have phones in their homes and we didn't even have long range radios because we did not have secret service vehicles. Special Agent Lapham came back to the house and shortly after ASAIC Behn arrived. We started making plans for the trip when a ranch hand showed up and he seemed to know about what LBJ had planned for the trip. The Vice President elect had two new white Lincolns there, one being a convertible and the hand said LBJ would drive the convertible and we could use the sedan as a follow-up car.

The convertible was placed in a convenient position for departure. I got behind the wheel of the sedan and positioned it about 15 feet behind the convertible. When the hunters came out they placed their equipment in the convertible. LBJ saw me preparing to drive the follow-up car and he came over and said to me "It's going to be real muddy where we are headed and it will be easy to get stuck. I think it would be better if my man here (ranch hand) drove this car because he is accustomed to driving in the mud." So I stood aside.

As we left to hunt just before 7:00 am, LBJ was driving the convertible with Senator Kennedy in the right front seat and ASAIC Behn in the backseat. I moved to the back seat of the sedan and Special Agent Lapham stayed in the front passenger seat, with the ranch hand driving. I still to this day can't believe that we were going deer hunting in cars instead of trucks and that this was a protective detail with two vehicles neither of which were being driven by an agent.

We drove several miles over to another ranch and down a lane to a house with a man standing on the porch. When we pulled up the man said "Lyndon, I rode over my place a while ago and I did not see any deer, and I don't know where they are." So, we went back out to the main road and drove several miles to another place and turned down what appeared to be a private road that had recently been worked by a bulldozer. The road was muddy and our wheels slipped frequently, but the ranch hand and LBJ kept their cars going without incident. There was nothing around as we drove a mile or two down the road until we came upon a large nice house with several outbuildings.

As we arrived, our host came out to meet our protectees. They had some conversation and then the host got in the back seat of the convertible with ASAIC Behn and pointed the direction for LBJ to drive. As we passed an outbuilding, our host summoned a cowboy in a pickup truck to follow us. The land was clear of any trees except for in a few low places where water might be found. The area we were driving through was very isolated and I had no idea where we were. Even if we had a radio, what would I have been able to tell the command post about our location? Absolutely nothing.

We traveled the recently bulldozed road up and down shallow grades until we came over a low rise and spotted a herd of deer standing on the side of the next hill. LBJ drove to within 200 feet of the deer and the deer just stood there looking at us. We waited while Senator Kennedy was given the first shot. The sound of the rifle going off made the herd take off, but one deer was partly down and a second shot brought it down. As we departed the host told the cowboy in the pickup truck "Load that deer and follow us." Then we were off again in search of more deer.

Within a short time we saw another deer herd, this time when we stopped LBJ killed a deer. We did this same type of movement in our little hunting caravan again so the host could kill a deer; each time the cowboy would load the deer in the truck and fall in place behind the cowboy driven follow-up car.

After the host had taken his deer, we saw the protectees talking together. Senator Kennedy turned around in his seat to better talk to our host in the rear seat. The host got out of the convertible and walked back to our follow-up car, approaching on my side, so I rolled down the window. The host said to me, "I have deer licenses for everyone and the cowboy has enough tags to put in the ear of the killed deer to include each of you so everything is legal if you want to join in this hunt. How about it, do you want to kill a deer? You can use my gun."

Now let me tell you how I made a big mistake that day. First let me say, I wanted to take this man up on his offer, I wanted to take a deer, but I hated to do it while the next President and Vice President of the United States were watching and waiting. I was an excellent shot, but using a gun I wasn't familiar with and the situation; I was working, I had protectees. Even though this was an unorthodox detail I was working...I made a quick decision and politely declined.

The host then leaned in the car so he could see SA Lapham and made him the same offer. Lapham immediately accepted. So out goes Lapham from the follow-up car, in comes the host and Lapham gets in the backseat of the convertible LBJ is driving. Two protectees in the front seat, one driving, two agents in the back seat...a cowboy driving the follow-up car and a special agent about to hunt a deer. LBJ took the lead again in the convertible and we drove until he spotted another herd of deer. Lapham got out of the car, took his shot and a deer with a nice rack hit the ground. This was the last time the cowboy had to load a deer in his truck, at least that day. We proceeded back to the ranch house of our host.

When we arrived our host came up to Lapham and asked for his name and address. "I'm going to get your deer meat processed, pack it in dry ice and ship it to you along with your deer head after the taxidermist gets done with it," our host told Lapham.

So you can see how I made a bad mistake that day. Lapham got the deer meat sent to his family, and the mounted head. I had neither. Big mistake!

This was around noon when we got back to the host's ranch house so he invited us in where we were served sandwiches, coffee and soft drinks. Afterward we returned to the LBJ ranch, arriving about 3:00 pm.

During all this time we had no way to communicate with our command post and they did not know where we were. For that matter, we didn't know where we were either! And it is the only time I have known of our highest ranking protectees riding in the same vehicle together with one of them driving, oh and let's not forget the cowboy driven follow—up car. I never heard any mention of the hunting trip in the news. We left early and came back when perhaps the press was not looking, so as far as I know there was never any publicity about the hunt. It certainly was an interesting day!

When SA Bob Lapham and I went into the command post at about 3:00 pm that day all we wanted was a place to sleep until we departed for Palm Beach. We had flown the day before, had very little sleep before we worked all night, then deer hunted all day. So Inspector Peterson and ASAIC Behn said we could lie on their beds which were nearby. They would wake us up in plenty of time to leave with the group.

About 6:15 pm the starting of an aircraft engine woke me up. I went to the window and the plane running an engine looked like the one we used to come to the ranch. I woke up SA Lapham saying, "We have to go now, our plane engine is running." We got on our shoes, grabbed our luggage, and hurried outside. We saw a large barn and a cow lot between us and the plane, and it was too far to go around so we climbed the fence and hurried toward the plane, dodging cow pies as we went. We had not seen any cows but when we got about half way across we saw a large bull standing near the barn and he was already watching us and pawing up dirt. Now that was scary! We had to climb the fence somewhere, so we ran toward the plane put our luggage over the fence and climbed out as fast as we could. We knew the bull was agitated but when he started snorting, it sure helped me over the fence!!!

My outer coat snagged on a barb or something and ripped. The aircraft crew saw us coming over the fence and held the plane for us. We just made it. The plane departed Stonewall, Texas about 6:30 pm and as before, with a small number of agents, I rode in Mr. Johnson's personal plane back to Bergstrorm Air Force Base, where we boarded the American Airline Charter for return to Palm Beach.

A few months later there was a report on the news and in the newspaper that Mr. Johnson's plane occupied only by the pilots, had crashed somewhere in the vicinity of Stonewall, Texas killing them both. How tragic![3]

---

3        Vice President Lyndon B. Johnson Daily Diary, Sunday, February 19, and Monday, February 20, 1961

# The Trip to Meet John John

On November 23, 1960, we flew with Senator Kennedy to Washington, D.C. so he could visit with Mrs. Kennedy who was already there and expecting a baby. Apparently nothing was happening so at 8:25 pm on November 24th we all boarded an American Airlines Charter and flew back to Palm Beach. I believe the plane was a DC- 4. When we landed the advance agent was SA Don Stringfield. As I was perhaps the first agent off the plane, he said to me "Forrest, grab these other agents and tell them not to leave, as you may be going back."

In his office, the airport manager was holding a call for Senator Kennedy and when the Senator came out he asked the manager and the plane captain, "How soon can we leave to go back?" It seems Mrs. Kennedy had gone to the hospital after we left Washington. The plane had to be refueled, cleaned inside, and restocked with food and supplies. They estimated 30 to 45 minutes to accomplish this. So about forty- five minutes later we left Palm Beach to return to Washington, D.C., at 12:50 am.

It was an uneventful flight until we were on final approach about 4:00 am to Washington National. I was seated by a window behind the wing on the right side of the plane. All of a sudden, the right inboard engine was covered in fire. This was the most frightening thing I have ever endured. We were flying between buildings in Alexandria, Virginia with the river beneath us. You could see the fire reflected in the water so the fire was on the top and bottom of the wing. I wondered how long the wing could stay in place or how long it would take for the fire to burn through the wing. There had been conversations going on and the press were their usual exuberant selves, but when the fire broke out the people in the plane became totally quiet and I thought I heard some praying. I was checking to see where the exits were, we crept lower and lower and the fire was burning as before.

As we finally touched down, fire trucks were racing alongside. Then the fire went out. The pilot stopped as soon as he could, still in the middle of the runway, and the fire trucks came up and covered the right wing in foam while the left two engines continued to idle. At a signal the pilot used the left two engines to taxi up to the gate and some very somber people disembarked. I never did want to crash and burn!! The motorcade was waiting and the "working shift", including me, accompanied Senator Kennedy to Georgetown University Hospital to see his son, John F. Kennedy, Jr., later known to the world as John John.

# The Kennedy Years

I was supposed to stay with the President Elect Detail until Inauguration Day, but I had an unfortunate occurrence in that I got the flu, the serious "lay down flu".

I was in the bed in a motel in Palm Beach for several days and when I got better, Jerry Behn came to me and he said, "Forrest, you're not over this yet. When you feel well enough, why don't you go home? I'll get somebody else to come down here." I was mobile, but I was weak so I went home on December 24th. It was about a month earlier than the date I was supposed to leave the detail.

Several months later, Vice President Johnson wanted to make a trip around the world. I was assigned with SA Larry Short to do the advance work on that trip in Manila, Philippines and Karachi, Pakistan.

I was in Karachi with Vice President Johnson's motorcade traveling along the edge of the city when we saw a group of Pakistani camel riders on the road up ahead. Vice President Johnson thought it would be interesting to talk to the camel riders.

He stopped the motorcade and one camel driver in particular is the one that he approached and started talking to through an interpreter.

119

This particular camel driver seemed to have a quick wit and through the interpreter, he and President Johnson established a relationship in the 15 or 20 minutes they talked. I don't remember all the circumstances about it, but Vice President Johnson had the interpreter find out who the fellow was and where he could be located.

Later on, after we got back to the States Vice President Johnson invited the camel driver to come to the United States. The camel driver did come to the United States and that particular visit, I think, influenced the camel driver's life quite a bit because next I heard of him, he was not driving a camel anymore, he was driving a truck. When we finished up that around-the-world trip, I went back to Birmingham.

In February or March of 1962, Mrs. Kennedy decided that she would take a trip to India and Pakistan. I was called about making advances on that trip.

A group of agents met in Washington, D.C. and we flew to New Delhi, India, where we received notice there had been a change in plans. We were told upon our arrival at the airport that Mrs. Kennedy had decided that she needed to spend another week in the U.S. before she made her scheduled trip, so we had a whole week off.

The Embassy was very generous with us, and they furnished us a car and driver. Three or four of us agents took various side trips. We made visits to other historical places around New Delhi, one of them being the Stainless Steel Pillar(see picture on page 101).

We visited some old forts that had been built by the rulers many years before. We saw several interesting places during that week.

We went to Agra, India where the Taj Mahal is located. That outing actually developed into one of the places where I was going to do an advance with Jerry Blaine.

The day before Mrs. Kennedy's trip to Agra I came down with a serious intestinal malady that we didn't have any medicine or cure for. So the day of Mrs. Kennedy's visit I went through the whole day without a drink of water or anything to eat because I was afraid of what the consequences might be. It was just one day anyway. I figured I could make it that long, and I did.

The next day Jerry Blaine and I flew out to Rawalpindi, Pakistan, aboard the Ernbassy's DC-3 aircraft. It was the first and only time I have flown on a DC-3. We were in Rawalpindi for several days before Mrs. Kennedy's visit. When I first went to Pakistan with Vice President Johnson in 1961 the capital was in Karachi, but they were in the process of moving it to Rawalpindi. When we got there a year later in 1962 for Mrs. Kennedy's stop the capital was Rawalpindi.

After our work was done we had an opportunity to visit a place called Murray, Pakistan which is a resort area in the mountains. We also visited the well known Kyber Pass, located between Pakistan and Afghanistan. We stayed in Murray a day or two and then we went to an ancient city that was being excavated called the City of Taxila. Blaine and I had a day off, so we got a car, an embassy driver and a security officer for a day of sight-seeing.

While traveling from Rawalpindi to Taxila we could see some low mountains off to our right that appeared to be composed of clay and the sides were shear. And as we looked closer we saw what appeared to be doorways that had been cut in the sides of these mountains and there were a number of them. Then we noticed that people were walking up pathways to the openings. The embassy guide said the best they could tell those caves had been lived in for centuries.

There was no air conditioning in our vehicle so we were riding with the windows down. We were going along and the driver pointed out the side of the car at a swarm of locusts. We quickly rolled up all the windows as the swarm engulfed us. The driver continued slowly, as I am thinking I am in a biblical scene...the swirl and destruction of locusts.

In Taxila, workers were digging up ancient artifacts. They had a big museum housing items they found. It was hard to believe the implements, cooking utensils, and other items they unearthed were, in many cases, the same type implements that the Pakistanis were still using. Some of the things that were dug up were approximately 2,000 years old and included a lot of coins.

We found a similar situation in India. People out in the villages were still living like we think people were living 2,000 years ago. In other words, life was not much different in the rural areas.

During our visit to Taxila, our driver-guide told us about a nearby well that has been in use for centuries by local residents. It is called "Alexander's Well". Legend has it that this well was actually used by Alexander the Great (356-323BC) during his march through the region.

We drove three or four miles and found the well located on a low-rise. We did not see any residences nearby, but while we were taking pictures, a man came up leading his donkey. The donkey was wearing a rack on which three earthenware water jars were tied, and he also had a tin bucket with a rope used to draw water from the well. Our Guide talked to the man who said he had traveled about three miles to get water, which he did two or three times a week. The man only knew that the well is said to be very old. (see picture on page: 91)

Karachi was Mrs. Kennedy's last stop. There the same camel driver met by Vice President Johnson the year before came to Mrs. Kennedy's residence and gave her and her sister a ride on his camel.

On March 27, 1962 I was assigned to assist Mrs. Kennedy's arrival at the Karachi Airport and security on the plane during our trip to London. Pakistan International Airlines, in addition to several older planes, had two new 707 jets they had been using for a short time and Mrs. Kennedy was flying in one of them. We learned that the jet pilots had been trained by Pan American Airlines, a U. S. carrier, and the planes were also being serviced and getting their fuel from Pan American Airlines, all of which gave us a feeling of *some* confidence.

That particular day Pakistan International Airlines assigned four captains as the flight crew on Mrs. Kennedy's plane, which arrived in Karachi partially loaded with passengers.

Mrs. Kennedy, accompanied by her sister, Mrs. Lee Radziwill had first class seats, Mrs. Radziwill had a window seat and Mrs. Kennedy sat next to her in the aisle seat. My seat was directly across from Mrs. Kennedy. We were scheduled to discharge passengers and refuel in Tehran, and stop in Paris before reaching London.

After take-off and reaching altitude, I went up to the cockpit and was allowed to sit in their spare seat and listen to the traffic. One captain was the pilot, a second was the co-pilot, the third was the engineer, and the fourth was for relief.

The radio traffic increased and the spare captain told me we were meeting their other jet, which was about two thousand feet below us en route to Karachi. The other jet was pointed out to me about 2,000 feet below but I only got to see it for a few seconds as the closing speed was about 1,000 miles per hour. Then the radio abruptly stopped as the planes flew out of radio range.

We flew into Tehran, discharged some passengers, and took on some fuel. After we left Tehran we were scheduled to stop in Paris, but after we were aloft the captains and the engineer began talking about the possibility they might have enough fuel to skip Paris and go directly to London. The engineer was calculating fuel usage closely and they finally decided they would call ahead to London and request a direct approach. They would only have a small amount of fuel left when they reached London if the request was granted and it was. I was happy when we safely reached London and I was released from the detail.

I remained in London overnight with SA Lem Johns. The next afternoon we boarded a flight to New York and then to Baltimore where I took a bus to Washington.

After I was back in Birmingham about a month I saw on TV and read in the newspaper that one of the two Pakistani jets crashed near Cairo, Egypt, killing all on board. I have never known if it was the jet we flew on or if any of our flight crew were on-board. Tragic!

Mrs. Kennedy's trip lasted about six weeks from February 16, 1962 to March 27, 1962. The trip was very interesting and I was glad that I had the opportunity to be part of it. I've pulled in a few of the pictures I took, but they are aging and some are now fading. I know how they feel.

# Back to Alabama

When I was coming to Washington from that trip overseas, we flew through London into Baltimore. The next day I went over and requested an interview with then-Director James Rowley.

Mr. Rowley had been Agent in Charge of the White House Detail while I was working there with President Eisenhower and during President Elect Kennedy's detail. He graciously gave me some of his time and when we met Mr. Rowley told me that the Service was going to establish a resident agency in Mobile, Alabama and that they had selected me to go there.

Of course, I had heard talk about the possibility of this before we left to go to India, but I didn't know who was going to be selected for the assignment. Word was I had been recommended to go there, but I didn't know that I'd be the one selected. At that time, I had been in the Service about nine years.

What a boost this was for me and for Marilou. I was pleased to be taking my bride and our children back to Alabama where we would all be closer to our family.

While assigned to the Birmingham Field Office, I would go down to Mobile, Alabama and work cases. There was a lot going on in the area, so in May of 1962 it was time for Marilou to start frying bacon in a new place.

While Marilou packed up our family and home for the move, I loaded the trunk of my government issued car with 450 case files and headed to open a small office in Mobile with a new promotion to Resident Agent.

I was in a one room office in the Federal building, with a desk, a couple of chairs, file cabinets, a phone and 450 cases that needed to be resolved. No secretary, no other agents; it was a bare bones operation, but with plenty of work to do.

At that time, there was a lot of emphasis on check forgery. Compared to now when check forgery is probably the least consequential thing that happens anymore with the Service. Back then it was a top priority.

Brookley Air Force Base was a major employer in the area. The employees at the base were predominately having their payroll checks mailed to their homes and they had been losing a tremendous percentage of those checks to mail thieves and forgers.

When I reached Mobile, the first instruction that I had was to call on the Commanding General, at the base, to let him know I was there and provide him some insight as to what plans we were making to apprehend the check thieves and forgers. I had been told the general was very much interested in his employees getting their checks on time. I did as instructed and got right to work on the investigations.

I worked closely with Postal Inspector, Zellie Brown, and early on we arrested a check thief and turned him into an informant. We postponed his case for a period of time and during that time he identified maybe 15 or 20 forgers, several with multiple acts of forgery. We uncovered three or four rings of check forgers that were implicated in a large portion of the crimes. This coupled with a lot of hard work really put a big dent in the crime there.

Often forgers would troll around for small merchants that would cash payroll checks without identification. All of a sudden that merchant would get loaded up with forged checks being charged back to his account. A few times, it was a pretty pitiful situation for the gullible merchant.

Let me explain how this worked before the digital age. A government check is cut and mailed to the payee. It is stolen, fraudulently endorsed, and cashed. The cashed check goes back to the Treasury records. An employee who didn't receive a check would contact their payroll office and be advised a check had been cut and cashed. The forged check is retrieved from files and sent out for investigation.

When we received a copy of the check from the Treasury our investigation would begin with the payee, or the endorser. Sometimes we found people with the same names who inadvertently received a check and cashed it. It ran the gamut, but most of the cases were outright crimes.

Counterfeiting was a priority of ours, and in fact protection of the currency was the original reason the Secret Service was created in 1865. This particular type of investigation was often complex and had many variables. We had to choose the right avenue to investigate or it could fall apart in an instant.

Predominately counterfeiters made $20 and $100 bills and they found ingenious ways to pass them into circulation. Bills would come in from a merchant or a bank because "somebody thought something just isn't right about it", and that was often the start of an investigation that might go *who knows where*. Sometimes the person who suspected the bill was counterfeit would write a car tag number on the bill or if they knew the person, write their name. Any information we could get helped develop leads to explore.

The territory I covered was part of the panhandle of Florida and some counties in southern Alabama. There were several counterfeit plants found in the area and we were successful in dealing with them and seized a large amount of counterfeit money.

After we arrested a number of multiple forgers we learned that most of them were addicted to the use of boiled paregoric. This was a controlled liquid substance sold by drug stores for use by mothers for their babies, when the babies have stomach problems and have trouble sleeping.

Pharmacists would only sell paregoric two ounces at a time, once per day, and they maintained a log book, trying to prevent overuse. The forgers got around that by getting someone to go into the drug store to buy it for them, or they went from store to store themselves.

The addicts would go to a place where they would fill a large steel kitchen spoon with the liquid paregoric. Next they would hold the spoon over a flame and let much of the liquid boil off, leaving the concentrated residue. Then using a needle, they would draw up the liquid and "shoot up."

If, for some reason, the addicts could not get enough paregoric or they got arrested while "high" and they had to "come down" they had severe withdrawal symptoms that could be alleviated only by drinking cane syrup...very odd.

After a few months, Inspector Tom Kelley, who had been in charge of the Washington, D.C. Field Office during my duty there and later became Assistant Director of Field Investigation for the Service, came through and determined that Mobile needed to be a full office because of the caseload. I would have the opportunity to build a team by getting an agent and an administrative secretary.

While Inspector Kelley was in the office one morning, a defendant we arrested about two years before showed up and requested to see me. He said he had been home from prison just a few days and had come by to tell me thanks for not mistreating him during his arrest and conviction. He felt he had been treated fairly and he appreciated it and wanted me to know. I asked him if he would tell the man next door, Inspector, Kelley, and he did. It seems some of his fellow inmates were telling bad stories about some of the officers who arrested them. It was the only time anything like that happened to me.

I anticipated that with Brookley A.F.B. closing there might be employees looking for work who were already Civil Service, and that's how I found my secretary, Mrs. Lucille Caudle.

Mrs. Caudle was married and had children, but they were all grown and out of the house. She was a great secretary and worked really hard to keep all our reports and communication flowing. Mrs. Caudle was also very good dealing with the agents, law enforcement, and the myriad of people that interact with The Service. The agent who transferred to Mobile was Special Agent Gary Seale from Birmingham, Alabama.

Later, when Mrs. Caudle's husband was transferred to San Antonio, TX, she was replaced by another Brookley AFB employee, Mrs. Ann Rouseau. Mrs. Rosseau was very capable and I was fortunate to have had such wonderful assistants.

One morning an informant came to the office, saying that I was becoming famous on the street and people knew me by name. He said that last night he was in a bar when a man came in that he knew only as "Iron Man", began drinking and bragging that Mr. Guthrie was looking for him. The informant said *Iron Man* hung out at two or three different places, and we should be able to find him.

Soon thereafter, Postal Inspector Zellie Brown and I gathered up copies of all the checks we were investigating and went and located Iron Man. He readily agreed to sit with us in the car and give specimens of his handwriting and while Zellie was getting the specimens I was looking through the copies for similarities.

I found three or four checks that looked good and asked Iron Man to write those names for us. They matched, Iron Man confessed and we arrested him.

Like I said, I never knew where an investigation would lead me. Well, here is an example. It is two weeks almost to the day after I moved to Mobile and opened the office. I had been working cases, some of which had already been under way from my trips down from Birmingham.

The evidence comes together on a case of counterfeit $20 bills being passed at several establishments in and around Mobile. A suspect has been described or personally tagged to the bills by witnesses. We obtained authorization for a search and uncovered his press and counterfeit bills.

This guy was the son of a city official. I felt sorry for the official, it wasn't his fault, but it was still his son.

# A Bale of Cotton Sitting in a Car

Where an investigation led me and who I might meet was always up for grabs. I just went where the proof took me and met whoever came along the way. One thing is for sure, I experienced more in my years investigating cases than I ever imagined would be possible to fit into a lifetime.

One very interesting counterfeiting case I worked while in Mobile began with merchants receiving several counterfeit notes and a description of a man, "that looks like a bale of cotton sitting in a car."

As I conducted the investigation it came to light how *Cotton* operated. He would drive to a grocery store or a drug store or a shopping center and park near the front door. When someone would walk by, Cotton would call them over and ask them to go in and buy an item for him and bring back his change. Cotton used his size and inability to get out of the car for sympathy from his unsuspecting partner in crime.

It worked not just a few times, but many times. Counterfeit notes were showing up in a few places and we were on his trail.

What *Cotton* would do is ask that some small item be purchased, but gave a counterfeit $20 bill to pay for the item. The $20 bill was fake but all the change he got back was real. *Cotton* would sit sometimes for hours in a shopping center and then move on.

We finally got enough evidence and proof to get a warrant to search *Cotton's* house and all his personal items. One afternoon Special Agent Gary Seale and I went to *Cotton's* house. It was in a higher crime area and there was safety in numbers, so we asked the local deputy sheriff to join us.

When we conducted the search we found more bills, just the evidence we needed to make an arrest. The deputy got the honor of placing *Cotton* into the backseat of his brand new 88 Oldsmobile, the whole backseat. After *Cotton* got in the back seat there was no room for Gary to sit.

Under a special section of the law dealing with counterfeiting, property used in the commission of the crime can be seized. I had the job of driving *Cotton's* vehicle to turn over to the Customs Bureau for storage while the seizure case was concluded.

When I got in the car the front seat looked normal, but I quickly found out otherwise. The seat flattened down to the floorboard. I had to find a crate to sit on to drive the car.

There was a procedure that had to be followed for everything I and my fellow agents did in the course of an investigation. There were forms that had to be filled out and reports filed. Document, document, document...it was the name of the game if we were going to have a solid case that could be prosecuted.

I never arrested people just to harass them, I arrested them because they had broken the law and I had proof. My investigations built the case. It was what the prosecution needed to get a conviction. It was my job to do it by the book and I insisted that anyone, regardless of the agency they worked for did the same.

Some of my work was non-criminal in nature. I conducted full field investigations on the background of candidates for a variety of government positions. A few times I investigated car accidents that involved a Federal employee to determine the government's liability.

During my six years in Mobile I also conducted some Protective Research Cases, which are threats to the President.

I guess you would say I was visible in the Mobile community and surrounding area. If the press was looking for information about a case or arrest in our areas of jurisdiction, I was one of the first people to get a call.

Often I could not comment on a case that was still under investigation or in trial. But when I could, my name, title with The Service and sometimes a picture would appear in the paper. Other agents were not authorized to make press releases.

I guess I would put it this way, and this applies to not only when I was in Mobile, but since the beginning of my time in the Service. I never hid that I was a Secret Service Agent, but I did not advertise it unnecessarily.

# The Assassination

President Kennedy was assassinated on November 22, 1963. I remember the exact day. My reaction to the assassination was disbelief and sorrow that the nation had lost its President. It was a tragic period for our country.

Within a few days of the assassination, l was called by Inspector Tom Kelley from Dallas. He requested that l drive to Mississippi to interview a person. I had to drive about 200 miles, but fortunately I was able to locate the person, do the interview and called Inspector Kelley in Dallas with the information.

I had one agent assigned at the office at that time named Gary Seale. Within two days of the assassination he was called to Dallas. He was assigned the job of security for Marina Oswald, because early on they didn't know what involvement she had with the event or what her contribution might be to an investigation. I believe they kept her in custody as a material witness.

When Gary finished that assignment, he was sent to Washington and they gave him a job in the Intelligence Division. He received investigative reports from not only the Secret Service, but from other Federal law enforcement agencies; as well as any report possibly connected to the assassination.

After the Warren Commission Report came out, things began to change for the Service. The major changes were in cooperation with the FBI and other Federal investigative agencies and local law enforcement. I know one time we received a memorandum from Headquarters that we were to type a personalized letter and mail it to every Chief of Police and every Sheriff of every city and county we covered requesting cooperation from them and asking that their departments please give the Service any information obtained in specific categories of threats.

My secretary, Mrs. Lucille Caudle, was a terrific person and a proficient typist. This was before computers and word processors. Everything had to be typed with a manual typewriter making a carbon copy. Mrs. Candle was turning out eight or nine of these personalized letters an hour and that was a lot. She was like a machine when she was typing. She'd take a little break now and then, but went right back to it.

If you recall, a few days after the assassination, our Service was initially making the investigation, but it was decided it would be better to have another agency do it so the investigation was turned over to the FBI.

We still made reports of interviews we had already conducted and sent them in.

Those were trying days for the Service. Every procedure, every agent, every movement, seemed to be under the microscope.

One thing that came out of that time, that I always appreciated, was The Service once-a-year would send out a little questionnaire that asked things like how we felt about our duties, how we felt about where we were living, and how we felt about our assignment, and if it was necessary to be reassigned to some other office, which office would you most prefer to be assigned to by preference 1, 2, 3.

Really and truthfully, this is how I left the White House Detail, because I never directly asked to leave the Detail. I think I was doing good work there because after I'd been away a year or two, I was given an opportunity to come back, but I didn't seize it.

You had these choices on the form and when I was in Washington, I'd always listed Birmingham as number 1, the Southeast as number 2, and I didn't do anything about number 3. I think that they finally got enough people to go to Washington or be on the Detail, so one day I found in my mailbox a transfer back to Birmingham and that's how my White House Detail days came to an end.

# Special Agent in Charge — Jacksonville, Florida

When I was in Mobile, I was putting Jacksonville, Florida as my number one next place. So one day, in 1967, it was probably the last of November or first of December I got a call from Mr. Peterson who was then Assistant Director of Investigations. He asked me if I really wanted to go to Jacksonville, that the man there, Joe Malkowski, was going to retire. I told Mr. Peterson I sure would be interested in going to Jacksonville and he said okay.

I went over to Jacksonville in December of 1967 to be in charge of the office on a temporary basis, but to be assigned there permanently on January 12, 1968. I was Agent in Charge there until I retired on September 30, 1977.

When I first arrived in Jacksonville, including me, we had an office staffed by six agents, three clerical employees, and thirty four counties in Florida to cover. We gradually grew to have me as SAIC, an Assistant Special Agent in Charge (ASAIC), twelve Special Agents, and five clerical employees. In addition we opened a Resident Agency in Orlando having three Special Agents and a clerk.

The growth of the Jacksonville office and the increase in the number of employees was brought about by the number of protectees visiting

Cape Kennedy (NASA) and Disney World, plus in election years, the campaigning of candidates for the office of President and Vice President. You see, even though I was no longer on full time Presidential details, when dignitaries came into my jurisdiction we still provided additional assistance and manpower.

We also had a number of newsworthy and attention getting counterfeit cases and at least one special case. It was perhaps the largest genuine silver coin smelting case in the history of The Service in which we seized about five and a half tons of melted silver bars and 800 pounds of genuine silver coins.

You might ask 'why'? At the time the silver content of older coins was worth more than their face value. This opened the door for numerous smelting operations around the country to extract the bullion, a practice which was illegal.

It may be interesting to note that at trial the government only entered about 300 pounds of melted silver into evidence as the courtroom floor was considered too weak to support five and a half tons; plus there was the logistical problem of moving five and a half tons to a secure place every night. At the time we estimated that $2.7 million in coins was smelted during the crime. The case resulted in six arrests and at trial, one acquittal and five convictions.

At the end of the trial, the melted silver and the genuine coins were delivered to the Internal Revenue Service. I never heard the true value the IRS received from selling the seized silver and coins.

Throughout my years in Jacksonville we had a heavy case load and we had several interesting protectees.

# We Have Liftoff

Jacksonville was really a very interesting office to be in during the time of the Apollo Space Missions. On January 27th, 1967, there was a cabin fire during a launch pad test of Apollo 1 and it killed astronauts Virgil Grissom, Edward White and Roger Chaffee. That tragedy put the program on hold for two or three years until NASA made changes and felt safe in resuming the Apollo program.

The first manned spacecraft that they sent up after the fire on Apollo 1 was Apollo 7, in October 1968. It was my good fortune to get to witness the launch of all of the missions from Apollo 7 through Apollo 15 from the front row because we always had a dignitary in attendance. One time we had four protectees down there to see the launch.

At the time of the launch of Apollo 7, Governor George Wallace was running for President and his running mate was General Curtis Lemay. General Lemay was in Orlando and he wanted to see the Apollo 7 launch, so we made the arrangements. We drove to the cape and NASA took us over and we watched from a roadway. After the rocket was fired, I thought it was really too close!!

There was nobody else on this roadway except us, and the VIP stands were somewhere about two or three miles away and I'm not sure how far we were away, but I know that NASA thought that we were at a safe distance. We could plainly see the rocket. When it went off, the roar and the static vibration was terrific. I don't know whether you know what static vibration is, but if you're standing up, these engines are so powerful that they emit sonic waves of energy. You'll notice that your pants are quivering and shaking. It's a tremendous thrill to witness a launch from that short distance. Until you've seen one, I don't know that I can totally describe the experience to you.

Apollo 7 was a successful launch, and after its success there were always some dignitaries present at every launch. I liked it and being Agent in Charge I had a certain amount of flexibility as to where I went in my territory. It became convenient for me to attend most of the time! Many dignitaries came down there and I probably can't remember all of them. Vice President Hubert Humphrey was there more than once. When he was in office, Vice President Spiro Agnew was there a number of times. President Nixon went there. We had King Hussein of Jordan there one time. At a different time, we had his wife, Queen Noor. President Nixon and VP Agnew attended the launch of Apollo 12.

We had one launch, Apollo 8, without a protectee, so after arrangements with NASA, I took our oldest son, Lane, to see the launch from the VIP stands. When we had a 'hold' in the countdown, we left our seats to stretch. While we were walking, I felt someone take my arm and say my name. It was Governor Claude Kirk of Florida and I was able to introduce Lane to him.

Another person we saw that day was actor Kirk Douglas. He was standing alone and when I saw him I thought he looked familiar. We approached and spoke. I told him he was a favorite actor of mine and we really enjoyed his movies. He was very congenial.

The night before the launch of Apollo 10, Vice President Agnew went over to the astronauts' quarters. They talked to him and us about the mission and they showed us certain slides of what they were planning to do. I can't remember which one of the three astronauts it was, but he was talking about what a thrill it was going to be when they approached the moon, as they were going to be upside down and they'd be watching between their legs.

The Apollo 11 mission landed on the moon, Vice President Agnew was there for the launch. We watched it from the launch control center through large glass observation windows. What an experience!! Later some of us received Certificates from NASA for being in attendance at the Apollo mission that landed on the moon.

All I can say is that it was a tremendous experience with the space program: seeing all the dignitaries. Foreign dignitaries came there as well as our own. In a letter I received at my retirement from Lee R. Scherer, the Director of the John F. Kennedy Space Center I was reminded of all the protectees we had during the years I was assigned to the Jacksonville office. Director Scherer wrote:

"Among those events you may recall participating in with us were the visits of Vice President Humphrey in 1963; several visits from Vice President Agnew in 1969, one of which coincided with our historic first mission to the Moon on July 16, 1969; and the joint visit of President Nixon and Vice President Agnew for the launch of Apollo 12 on November 14, 1969. Also the Heads of State visits of such dignitaries as Chancellor Willie Brandt of Germany, Prince Juan Carlos and Princess Sofia of Spain, and King Hussein of Jordan may be as memorable to you as they are to our own participants."

# It's A Small World

Disney World in Orlando opened in 1971,within two weeks we had a foreign dignitary there. From time to time, there were foreign dignitaries from other countries that heard about Disney World and just had to see it.

I can't remember the names of a lot of them but some were from smaller countries. King Hussein of Jordan was there a time or two. There was a fellow named Samosa who was the President of Nicaragua. There was a fellow there that was the President of a couple of islands in the Caribbean. There were dignitaries from all over the world. I'd have to go back through various records to find the names, but they were all protectees and somebody had to go down there to show them around.

The protectees would go on the rides. Disney had wheel chair entrances to all these places and arrangements were made for the protectees to go in that way and take a seat before they let the public come in at the normal entrance. Of course, we always had our place staked out. The security people at Disney World, soon found out what we liked, and of course, they always had helpful suggestions to handle various situations in the park. I would have to say that those protectees had a really good time.

I'll tell you another little instance that happened. King Hussein was there one time and stayed a week or more. He visited the park two or three times, but while he was there, Boeing Aircraft delivered him a new plane. I believe it was a 747 from the state of Washington. It had been on order for awhile and the King waited in Orlando for its delivery. You see, King Hussein was a certified jet pilot and wanted himself and his crew to fly the plane home themselves.

The thing about it was he had never been on that plane until he went out there at night to take off to go home. I guess perhaps his crew had flown it around Orlando a little bit to familiarize themselves with it. At any rate, we always waited on the ground 20 or 30 minutes after one of our protectees got in the air just to make sure there wasn't a situation that would require them to make an immediate return.

Orlando was a busy commercial airport and the Air Force shared runways. King Hussein's pilot fired the plane up and they taxied out. I am not sure what communication took place for clearance to go on the runway, but at any rate what happened next was out of our control.

He taxied onto the end of the runway and started his takeoff roll, but there was an incoming big jet on final approach on the same runway. Fortunately, the captain of the incoming jet saw what was happening and he put on all the power he had. With his wheels still down, he took off again over King Hussein's plane. I bet be didn't clear him by 200 feet.

We almost saw a huge crash in the making, and if it hadn't been for that incoming pilot seeing what was happening and reacting promptly, there would have been a big tragedy there.

On one occasion, the Shah of Iran came to Jacksonville and King Hussein of Jordan was somewhere else in Florida. When he found out about the Shah coming to Jacksonville, he wanted to come up and meet him and he did. It seemed that the Shah was interested in buying some military equipment, maybe some aircraft from the United States. It was arranged through the State Department for the Navy to put on a flight demonstration for the Shah and King Hussein, at Cecil Field, which was a Navy base in Jacksonville. It was one of the most interesting sights that I've ever seen because I think they exhibited three different airplanes, F-14, 15 and maybe a 16.

They had these aircraft perform against an F-4 Phantom which was an older Delta wing aircraft that in its day was a fine airplane and it was fast. We understood that the Shah had a number of F-4's in his Air Force. The Navy put on some flight demonstrations. One of the things they did, was for an F-4 to line up with one of the F-14's on the runway like they were going to drag race, seeing who could get off the ground first. The Phantom was still on the ground trying to take off when the F-14 was up in the air and came around and made a strike on the Phantom, as it had not left the ground yet.

Another demonstration had a man standing in the middle of a field approximately the size of a football field. An F-14 could make a pass over the field and the man started running and he could not get out of the way before the plane turned around and came back and fired on him while he was still in the open .

When the flight was over, the Shah wanted to talk to the F-4 pilot. The pilot landed and was approaching the Shah in the viewing stands when the Shah said, "Did you make your plane do all it would do?" The pilot answered, "Yes, sir."

I know those pilots were wearing G suits or whatever it is they do, but I surely didn't know the planes were capable of the flying they exhibited. Nor did I know the human body could take that kind of punishment, but they showed that they could. That's the most interesting flight demonstration I ever saw.

President Sadat of Egypt came to Jacksonville on November 2, 1975, and President Ford came down to meet him. President Sadat stayed at the home of Mr. and Mrs. Raymond Mason.

President Ford stayed at the home of an automobile dealer in Jacksonville named Luther Coggin and some activities were at the home of Mr. and Mrs. William Drennen. That was a pretty interesting summit. As a matter of fact, when President Ford was arriving at the Coggin home, the Navy had a helicopter that was doing an aerial surveillance and he was supposed to stay a certain distance away so that the noise didn't interfere with the President.

The plan was to land the helicopter on the golf course not far from the Coggin home. I happened to be looking when something obviously went wrong. The pilot put the helicopter in a tight turn and he could not recover from it. The body of the helicopter was going around in circles. The pilot was trying to control it but it would make a fast circle and slow down at one point, and then it would make another fast circle and slow down at that same point again.

I don't know what caused the problem, but the helicopter was 300 or 400 feet above the ground when this started. The helicopter was out of control but the pilot was attempting to get it down. He still had good engine speed, but he didn't have control of the body of the aircraft. When he was letting it down, he saw that in the direction the aircraft was headed was a strip of pine trees between the fairways of the golf course. When he saw that, he had to power the helicopter up over the pine trees, but the body of the helicopter was still rotating along with the blades.

It's not rotating fast, but I'm sure it was enough to give a passenger a real thrill. When the pilot got over the pine trees, he cut power and the helicopter landed. The skids hit the ground with such force from the side that, I believe, it was the co-pilot's boots that went through the plexiglass of the helicopter, and the pilot, it seems like one of his feet went through the plexiglass also.

We had an agent riding in the helicopter named Paul Magowski. He was strapped in at an open door so I know he was having a thrilling ride. Fortunately no one was injured. Nobody went to the hospital that day, but the next day the Commanding Officer (CO) of the Navy base called me and asked me to have Magowski come out so he could get a physical evaluation by a Navy doctor.

At that time, I asked the CO for a report of the investigation of the helicopter accident. I don't think it was ever determined what caused the problem.

# Julie Nixon-Eisenhower Protection Detail

President Nixon's daughter Julie married David Eisenhower, grandson of President Dwight Eisenhower. David was an Ensign in the U. S. Navy aboard the Albany, a missile cruiser, and was being transferred to Mayport Naval Station.

One afternoon in late June, 1971, I received a call from Special Agent Hal Thomas, an agent with the White House Detail. He advised me about the transfer, and said that the next day he would accompany Mrs. Pat Nixon and Julie Eisenhower aboard a small jet to Mayport Air Station. They were coming for the purpose of locating a suitable apartment for David and Julie. Further, that a realtor had been engaged to line up apartments for them to view. This would be an "off the record" trip.

The next day I drove to Mayport and met the plane. SA Thomas rode in the right front seat, and Mrs. Nixon and Julie rode in the rear seat as we followed the realtor to the first location, a small house on the ocean.

I stayed outside while the others went in to look. There was a large tree in the front yard which had several cactus plants growing there and the tree provided the only shade. A few minutes later Mrs. Nixon came out and stood under the tree with me. She was very cordial and perhaps she remembered having seen me on other occasions. She was talking about her family and the move to Mayport. Then she noticed the cactus and went over to look more closely.

She said that when she was a small girl living in California, her family had cactus like those growing in their yard and that by pulling the ears off and cleaning off the stickers, the ears could be fried and eaten. I was not aware that cactus were edible until then.

Next we proceeded to a garage apartment located behind a large oceanfront home on Beach Avenue, Atlantic Beach. This unit was either new or recently renovated and was located over a large garage and included suitable ground floor space we, the Secret Service, could rent and use as an office for Julie's protective detail. This was the apartment chosen.

I returned my passengers to Mayport and they returned to Washington. Then on July 19, 1971, Ensign and Mrs. David Eisenhower moved into their new home. Mrs. Eisenhower was employed teaching the fourth grade at Mayport Elementary School.

Later on February 16, 1973, President and Mrs. Nixon returned to Mayport and motorcaded to Mr. and Mrs. David Eisenhower's apartment. They spent time visiting them, greeting their neighbors, and the President made a short speech to a crowd that had gathered quickly when it became known the President was there.

The sixteen story Pablo Towers Apartment to house the elderly at Jacksonville Beach was dedicated on August 17, 1973 by Mrs. Julie Eisenhower. Julie was a really nice, considerate person to work with.

# King at the Stick

King Hussein of Jordan came to Florida several times over the years. Two specific occasions I recall are when King Hussein came to Orlando to visit Disney World for two or three days and the time he came to see a moon launch at Cape Canaveral. Now that trip, I will never forget.

After the launch, we took King Hussein back to Kennedy Space Center air strip where his plane was parked. You see King Hussein was a pilot, so it wasn't uncommon to see the king' s plane arrive with him at the stick. This day was no exception, he was going to take command of the plane and fly to the next destination in his journey, Miami. King Hussein's plane was parked near several other aircraft in an area in the shape of a circle. He got ready to depart, and when the time came for the King to taxi out of the area, there was a flagman on the ground directing him out.

Another empty plane was parked nearby and the king obviously saw it was close, but the ground guide just kept waving him forward. That was a mistake because the wingtip of the King's plane was at the same level as the wingtip of the parked plane, and right there in front of everyone, King Hussein's wingtip hit and split the other plane's wingtip. Although the King stopped his plane immediately, the two planes were now joined.

The plane ramp came down and the King came with it. The King loudly announced that he was the pilot of the plane and that he took full responsibility for the incident. He specifically absolved the flag-man when he said "Don't let anyone bother that man about what just happened." To me this showed the King was a "stand-up" man of character. The King said that he needed a plane to continue his trip to Miami.

Our detail leader was standing with the King, and we both knew we had to figure out how to handle this situation quickly. I saw the base commander of Patrick Air Force Base standing in a group of people near the area. I told the King I would see what I could do. I went and talked to the general and he said the King could use his aircraft. It was at Patrick Air Force Base, but he would get a crew together as soon as possible, which might take a while because it was a Sunday. I thanked the general and went back to tell King Hussein and our agents that a plan was in action.

The general started making phone calls and soon came to tell me his aircraft was being prepped, a crew was being assembled, and he had ordered a repair crew from Patrick AFB to come and see about separating the plane wings. The repair crew arrived before the general's aircraft and immediately began removing the tip from King Hussein's plane, drilling out the rivets. As soon as the general's plane arrived the King and his party boarded. There were not enough seats on the general's aircraft to accommodate two of the agents on the King's protective detail, but the King's aircrew said as soon as their wingtip was removed, they would resume their flight to Miami and the agents could go ahead and fly with them.

The agents came to me and said "Mr. Guthrie, can you get a ride for us to the airport in Orlando so we can fly commercially to Miami?"

They said they did not want to fly in that plane without a wingtip as they thought it was too dangerous. These were agents that never exhibited any fear about anything they did, but truthfully, I shared their concern about the plane. So I told them I would try to find out if this was a good idea or not by asking an Air Force Colonel pilot standing with the general. The colonel said, "The King's aircraft and the crew will not notice the missing wingtip. It is not a significant fault that jeopardizes the safety of the aircraft." With this information the agents decided to fly on the King's plane after all. Once the crew got the tip loose, it was loaded on the aircraft along with the agents and the plane took off for Miami.

*Forrest Guthrie*

# George Wallace

George Wallace was running for President in 1968. I had just moved to Jacksonville from Mobile. On the campaign trail he flew in an old DC-6. When he arrived in Jacksonville, the ground crew went out with oil catcher pads and placed them under each one of the engines due to oil leaks. I wondered ...how old is this plane?

When the stop in Jacksonville was over and he came back to his plane, the people who had helped with the trip and the firemen and policemen, would line up by the stairs to his plane and he would shake each hand and thank them for helping. When he got to me, he said "I remember you, you are from Mobile, Alabama. One time we had pictures made together in my office in Montgomery and I auto-graphed one and mailed it to you. It is nice to see you again."

He congratulated me and wished me well on my promotion and move to Jacksonville. He had campaign stops in Florida and several in our Jacksonville area. He was always friendly and personable.

# This is Andrew

In February 1976, the Service began seeing a previously unknown and deceptive $20 note being circulated in the Denver area. An initial investigation was unproductive. The passer moved on to New Orleans, and later to Mobile where a pattern developed. The passer would try to sell counterfeits to used car dealers, mostly to ones located on "automobile" row. He used the name "Andrew". No one had seen Andrew as he called on the telephone and used an innocent messenger to deliver his notes.

Thinking that the counterfeiter might be coming to Jacksonville, I asked SA George Hulcher to canvass our major used car dealers located on North Main Street in Jacksonville and request them to let us know immediately if they heard from "Andrew" with his money making plan. It wasn't long after that when a manager, at one of the local car dealerships SA Hulcher had visited, got a call from "Andrew". The manager told "Andrew" he was interested, but it would take him a day to get the money together, so call him back at 11:00 am to make arrangements the next day. The manager of the dealership hung up with Andrew and called our office immediately.

The timing couldn't have been worse because all of the agents assigned to our area were protecting candidates who were on the campaign trail in and around Florida. I knew I would need some extra help when we got the call from the manager that Andrew had been in touch. I called headquarters and asked that additional agents be sent to help with a stakeout.

In the meantime, I was able to gain information about a possible location that Andrew was calling from. It turned out to be a phone in the lobby of the Robert Meyer Hotel, right across the street from our Jacksonville Field office. This tip was too hot to let wait until other agents arrived, so I went on my own to investigate. On my way out the door I asked the secretary to find any agent she could or the next one that walked in the door and send them to assist me.

I found about 20 pay phones in the lobby of the hotel. One bank of them was located down in an alcove around a corner...a little more private and tucked away. I took up a position, reading a newspaper and looking like any other downtown businessman reading in the lobby of a hotel. After a while, two men came into the lobby, one an older gentleman and one younger. They looked like father and son possibly. The two men talked for a while, when one broke off and went into a phone booth in the alcove. I went into the booth next to him and acted like I was going to make a call. I waited to hear the caller's conversation, "Hello this is Andrew," were his first words.

I hung up may phone and walked out of the booth. Okay, this is Andrew, but there are two of them and only one of me. What's next? About this time SA Butch Windham walked into the lobby of the hotel. I walked up to Windham and said, "Andrew is here and he has a friend. If they split and run, you take the younger one." Andrew and his accomplice walked out of the hotel lobby and started across the street through Hemming Plaza, a small downtown park. It was then that SA Windham and I approached the two, showed them our books (credentials) and I told them I would like to have a conversation about counterfeit money. "Our office is right upstairs, will you come with me?" The older man said, "Yes sir, we will go."

We took Andrew and the other suspect upstairs to our office and placed them in and interrogation room where I started by asking to see any money they had in their wallets or pockets. Both suspects gave me what they had and sure enough some bills were the counterfeit note we had been tracking. I told the suspects that I knew their money was counterfeit, but that it was some of the best work I had ever seen. "Is one of you the printer?" I asked. The older man said, "Yes, I am the printer. My son and I fell on some hard times and we started printing bills. We never should have done it."

From that moment forward the two of them were interrupting each other in their stories and accounts to tell me all they knew about their counterfeiting operation. Each of them had packages and bags from purchases they had made earlier in the day in the downtown area. Agent Windham used the receipts to return to each store and retrieve the counterfeit notes used to make the purchases. We also found more counterfeit notes in their hotel room. In the end they were both arrested and so were others related to the case.

The work we had done to warn local car dealerships about this scam was key to getting Andrew and his son off the streets. Fortunately, we also had a good manager who called us right away when he heard from Andrew. I have often thought about that day and each time realize that it all could have gone very different. You see at that point in my career as the Special Agent in Charge I wasn't out working cases, but because all my agents were on protection details, I was the only agent available to respond. When word got out about how the arrests happened I received a letter of commendation from Headquarters.

# The Service

I retired from The Service on September 30, 1977 after 25 years. After that, Marilou and I took our Winnebago and we made several trips, mostly to the western part of the United States. We visited national parks and historic landmarks.

When I compare the country of today versus the country of my youth, times have indeed changed. Transportation is so much better and faster. Cars are so much more reliable. There are good roads on which to drive those cars and food available along those roads. Bathrooms too!

If I knew someone that was starting as a new agent, my advice would be to always conduct yourself in a professional manner. While you're working, leave frivolity somewhere else. Learn all there is to know about your job. Always do your job to the best of your ability. Never take any assignment lightly. Some assignments that you may get initially may not seem worth the time to you, but never forget that some older and wiser and more experienced agent has requested you to do this and they didn't do it without a good reason.

I would say always be considerate of others and consider that if you're on a Protective Detail, you're the uninvited guest there, and that your job is to do your work as inconspicuously as possible. As inconspic-uously as the job might let you be inconspicuous. Sometimes you have to be standing out front, but a lot of the times you don't. That's probably as much as I have to say about The Service.

I'll tell you one thing, it was an extremely interesting and rewarding career for me. Like I said in the beginning, I knew the day that I found out about the Secret Service, it was the only career I wanted. I don't know what I would have done for a career if The Service had not taken me on, and now that it's over, I'd just like to say that I really wish it never would have ended.

# A Retired Agent's Tour of The White House

In the fall of 1988 Marilou and I attended the Association of Former Agents of the U.S. Secret Service (AFAUSS) annual meeting held near Washington, D.C. It was the last year of Ronald Reagan's presidency and I had not been in the White House for 12 or 15 years. Some people expressed an interest in seeing it, so we chartered a bus that took a group of us who had served on Presidential Details to tour the White House.

The head usher that greeted everyone coming in to the White house that day had been an agent. His name was Rex Scouten. As we were touring rooms in the east wing, Mrs. Nancy Reagan opened the door and stepped in. "I am so happy you are all here!" She said. The next thing we knew, Mrs. Reagan took over the tour and with a great knowledge of the history and traditions of the iconic American place she and President Reagan had called home for seven years.

Before our tour ended, a White House photographer appeared and Mrs. Reagan said, "I would like to have my picture made with each of you, so we can remember this special day." Each of us took a turn having an individual picture made with Mrs. Reagan. She was a very gracious and interesting hostess and that was a very remarkable day for me.

This was the last time I was in the White House.

# Veteran of the Day

Disney World has continued to be a favorite place to visit over the years for my family and me. On August 1, 2007 my wife Marilou, son Kent, and I made another of many tours of the Magic Kingdom. We had enjoyed the day and were intending to leave the park. About 4:30 pm walking down Main Street toward the entrance at the train station, I spotted a Disney employee eyeing us as we approached. When we got closer she wanted to know if we would talk to her for a moment. She said her name was Diana Shepard Martin and she asked if I was a veteran. (I presume she had noticed my balding head with a grey fringe of hair made it a good chance I was a veteran.)

Diana explained that she needed a veteran to participate in their flag lowering ceremony at 5:00 pm and if I was a veteran, would I help? I explained to Diana that I was a World War II Veteran, having been discharged as a Staff Sergeant in the Army MP's in 1946. I would be pleased and honored to participate.

The flag lowering ceremony is like everything Disney does, first class. They have three uniformed men for the ceremony which is conducted with military precision accompanied by the Disney World Band playing patriotic music, with the veteran included there are four people in the ceremony.

As the flagpole is located at the main entrance of the Magic Kingdom and a number of people are leaving for home at 5:00 pm, a large number usually wait for the ceremony. I was introduced to the captain of the team and about 4:50 pm we did a familiarization walk.

Then at 5:00 pm we marched across the street and lowered the flag. The other three gentlemen in the detail folded it, the flag was presented to me and we marched it across the street to the point of our beginning. The only thing that marred the ceremony was that a little rain started right at 5:00 pm and we got a little damp. We finished our job with precision, ignoring the dampness.

At the end, I was presented with a certificate, two or three Disney pins, and photographs made by the Disney photographers, all naming me as Veteran of the Day. Of all my trips to Disney World in the past 40 plus years, this was the most memorable one. What an honor to be Veteran of the Day and participate in this large public event!

# More to the Story

As was mentioned at the beginning of this work, I had very humble beginnings in rural Alabama, having been born in 1927. I lived through the depression as a child and can only marvel at how far the country has come from those times. At that time no one knew if the country would ever recover, so it was a very trying time much like our most recent downturn.

Join me now in a flashback to what it was like during that time and how events unfolded which led to my becoming a Secret Service Agent and ultimately a Special Agent in Charge (SAIC).

# Alabama Boy

You've heard people say they come from humble beginnings, well in my case it isn't just something I say. It is what I lived growing up in rural Alabama during the depression.

Times were hard for many people and my family was no exception. Usually my family had what we needed, living on the edge of town with a cow and a few chickens for milk, eggs, and meat. There were times, however, when all we had was buttermilk and cornbread for a meal.

What I did always have was a mother and father who loved me and worked very hard along with a little sister that thought I hung the moon. That was a lot more than many children of the depression had, so I was lucky!

I never dreamed in those days all the experiences I would have. I was just a little boy from Alabama, with a whole lot to see and a big world to experience.

# Dad, Mom, Me, and Marian

I was born Forrest G. Guthrie in April, 1927 in a home my parents, Forrest and Carrie Guthrie rented in Tallassee, Alabama.

My parents had married in 1922 and were both school teachers. Daddy taught biology, chemistry, and physics in high school. He was also qualified to teach history. Momma was an award winning teacher who taught predominately third and fourth grade.

I had one sister, Marian, born in January, 1930 in a small four room house with a garden that my parents rented on the south side of Eclectic, Alabama. Actually one of my first memories is the day my sister Marian was born.

Nobody had said anything about a baby coming and at three years old I was too young to notice or understand that momma was pregnant. That chilly day in January, I went to spend some time with the neighbor lady down the street.

The neighbor and I had a big time that started with a trip to the store in her black Ford Model-T. While we were in the store, I saw a bunch of bananas and the neighbor bought one for me. What a treat! This was a memorable day already when my dad came and took me home.

I remember walking in the door and seeing momma lying in bed holding Marian. It is something I will never forget.

I remember that we didn't have much, but there were others who had even less. Because we lived on a main highway, several times people came to our door asking for work or a handout.

"Mister, do you have any work I could do to earn some money or get a meal?" That's what I heard the travelers ask my Daddy when they knocked on our door around dinner time. Sometimes it was in the middle of the day while we were working in our garden, someone would come up in hopes of finding work or something to eat.

Like I said we didn't have much, but I never saw my parents turn anyone away empty handed. Even when there was nothing in the cupboard to send with them, or nothing to fill another plate, my parents gave to others what they could.

I remember on more than one occasion my Dad said in response to the request for work or food, "See that field across the road? I own it and the crops on it. Go get yourself some corn or watermelon. Only what you can eat while standing there. The rest I need to feed my family. God be with you in your travels stranger."

Every year when summer came my parents were not teaching, so they had no income. Daddy decided he was going to become a vegetable peddler. He would go to the neighbors who had surplus vegetables like corn, peas, beans, tomatoes, watermelon, and chickens, and buy the produce from them. Then Dad would travel all over Tuskegee, Tallassee, and Notasulga in an old 1920's Chevrolet held together by bailing wire, selling his produce. He developed routes and had some consistent customers.

Many times I would go with Dad on his route, sometimes he even let me sit on his lap to help drive. One day, when I was about six years old, I was driving on Dad's lap headed home. The roads were muddy and we were passing a farmer's wagon parked along a road.

We had a chicken crate attached to the sideboard (Dad sold live chickens and eggs when he could get them). I steered too close to the farmer's wagon and the next thing I knew the crate had hit the hub on the wagon wheel and the side of the crate burst open. Dad yelled

"Forrest, we have to stop, and keep those chickens from getting out of the crate."

When we got out and looked into the crate the chickens were all huddled up in a group against the back of the crate paralyzed with fear. It was like a cartoon. Dad flipped the crate around so the hole was against the car and strapped it back on the side board and off we went.

You know that farmer never seemed to notice or care about what was going on, he just kept working his field.

In 1933 both my parents got jobs teaching in Calhoun County, Alabama at a place called Sulphur Springs near Lincoln. Daddy bought 120 acres of land, about 100 acres of which was woodlands. He made a deal with a man who owned a portable saw mill to cut enough timber to build a house for our family and take his pay in timber.

Daddy, Grandpa John (momma's dad), and Uncle Hollis (momma's brother) built us a house while we lived in a rented house nearby. The rented house was a drafty little place out in the country with wood shingles. The only heat was from a fireplace and an iron cooking stove in the kitchen. During the winter we spent in the rented house, snow seeped in through the gaps in the walls and doors. Dad cut wood from our land so there was always plenty of fuel to stay warm as best we could and Momma made sure we had plenty of quilts to bundle up.

It was while we were living there, about 20 miles from Anniston, Alabama, that I faced one of my greatest challenges. I became seriously ill with a "cold", a sore throat, and bronchitis. I woke up one morning struggling to breathe. I woke up my parents and when they saw my difficulty they discussed it hurriedly. In 1933 no medical care was available. My mom went to the kitchen and got a spoonful of sugar, while my dad got a small bottle of turpentine. They put 3 or 4 drops of turpentine on the sugar and told me to swallow the mixture. I did the best I could. The effect was surprisingly immediate. The turpentine opened me up and I gradually got better. I think that country remedy saved my life. Note: Please do not try this country remedy at home, as turpentine may not be safe to ingest.

Wash day was tubs of water drawn from the well, either homemade lye soap or Octagon soap, and a rub board. A large iron pot, on three legs, was kept in the yard to boil the clothes clean. It always took extra time to build a fire around the pot to keep the water hot. After the clothes were rinsed in a tub, they were hung out to dry on lines. Mother tried to wait for a suitable day as the washing and drying had to be done outside....no such thing as a dryer yet either!

Sometime in 1940, I believe it was after the war had started in Europe, mother was able to buy her first washing machine. It was a big improvement and time saver. The machine was a brand named 'Easy' and Momma agreed!

Perhaps I didn't realize how hard times were. That is until one time when my parents got paid with a voucher for their months of teaching. My parents would normally receive a check from the county for their wages, but this time, it was a voucher. Mom and Dad would get paid when the county had the money.

That wasn't going to work, so Dad found a country store that would take the vouchers and give us half of what the value was in items from the store. My parents sure worked hard to only get half of what they earned.

# "My People"

If you ask where I come from that means you are asking me to tell you about "My People." My parents, my grandparents, great grand-parents, siblings and off-spring throughout the generations are "My People." They all come from basic, humble roots. Most of them were farmers. Daddy's parents, Benjamin and Lizzy Guthrie were married in 1893 when Granny Lizzy was just 16. They had a farm between Notasulga and Tallassee, Alabama where they raised cotton, corn, and vegetables.  My Dad was one of 11 children. Grandpa Benjamin, was the son of James  Guthrie and Samantha Guthrie. She was half Creek Indian.

Great Grandpa James and Great Grandma Samantha were married in 1859. My Grandpa Benjamin was the eighth of 13 children from their marriage, but he was actually one of a total of 23 children fathered by Great Grandpa James.

You see, Great Grandpa James had been married before to Sarah Barnett from 1840 until her death in 1859 They lived in a community south of Dadeville called Center Port, Alabama and had 10 children together. Sarah and their 10th child died during childbirth.

Great Grandpa James was a farmer and he was also a circuit riding

Methodist Minister.  He served three or four churches every Sunday riding his horse to services at one church for services starting at 9:00 am, then on to the next church for services at noon and a break for lunch with the  congregation.  Then he would travel to the next church for another sermon.

There are stories that could be told about all my father's siblings, but the lives of two always stood out to me. Probably because of how different the two were and how each of them affected my life.

I must have heard the story about Uncle Pinky a hundred times. His real name was Pinkney. I never met Uncle Pinky because he died when he was 8 or 9 years old, long before I was born. It was the story used to remind all of us children as we were growing up what could happen if you didn't do as you were told by your parents.

Uncle Pinky liked to lie down on the porch and eat peanuts. Everyone told him several times not to do it, but he continued. One evening Uncle Pinky was enjoying some peanuts on the front porch and he got one stuck in his wind pipe.

The closest hospital was in Montgomery, Alabama, 40 miles away. They took Pinky by train to Montgomery but he died on the table while the doctor was trying to remove the peanut.

Like I said, I never met Uncle Pinky, but the story of his brief and tragic life always played in my mind. As I made decisions through life, I thought to myself, is this the right thing to do or am I lying on the porch eating peanuts?

The other of my father's siblings that had a powerful impact on my life and I remember vividly is my uncle Virgil Guthrie. Unlike Uncle Pinky, I knew Uncle Virgil for a good part of my life.  I watched him, I heard his stories, and I learned many things from him.

Uncle Virgil was born on February 1, 1897 in a little cabin in Tall-apoosa County, Alabama about one mile from where Martin Dam is now located. He was four years older than my father and attended the Guthrie School, named for their grandfather, J. E. Guthrie.

At a young age, Uncle Virgil moved with his family to a farm near Reeltown where he attended school until he completed the tenth grade on March 24, 1916. On September 5, 1917 Uncle Virgil was drafted into the United States Army and went to Camp Pike to be inducted for service in World War I. While at Camp Pike he was taken sick with the flu that was such a great epidemic all over the world. He almost died in a hospital that was overcrowded with patients. As Uncle Virgil told it, he finally recovered enough, just in time to be shipped overseas on the last boatload of soldiers sent into the pit of devastation of World War I.

Always the industrious fellow who was savvy about money, Uncle Virgil used his Atlantic crossing to make a bit of pocket coin. He went to the supply commissary and bought apples for five cents each and sold them to other sailors, two for fifteen cents. He landed in Brest, France on November 19, 1918 with money in his pocket, but nowhere to spend it.

After a few days in Brest, his unit moved on to Le Mons where he had to sleep on the ground in the snow. Uncle Virgil had been issued three blankets; one to sleep on and two for cover.

One night he decided to explore and went into a tent where soldiers were sleeping on cots. In a corner he found a cot that was broken down in the middle. Uncle Virgil claimed until the day he died that was the best night of sleep he ever had, that night inside a tent, off the frozen ground.

Virgil went on to Tours, and finally stopped in Malicorne where he guarded German prisoners of war for six months. Next it was off to Gievres, a big supply base with several warehouses. Here too, for three months, Uncle Virgil guarded prisoners of war.

One experience he often talked about was when he left Gievres and went to Koblenz, Germany along the Rhine River. He made the trip with other American soldiers and German prisoners of war. The trip to Koblenz was by way of Le Johns which was about twenty five miles inside Germany.

In Le Johns all the German prisoners of war were released. During the entire journey Uncle Virgil had traveled in freight box cars, so when he crossed the Seine River and went around Paris, not once, but twice, he didn't see or experience a thing.

Uncle Virgil landed back on American soil in New Jersey on October 12, 1919. From there he was brought to Camp Gordon, Georgia where he was discharged on November 3, 1919, fourteen months after his enlistment.

The family was glad to have him back home. He was called from the fields of Alabama to render service to his country. To the fields he returned when the service was complete.

In 1920, Uncle Virgil bought a mule and planted some land in cotton and corn. He made two bales of cotton which he sold for about $100. In 1926, he bought a two mule riding cultivator, which was an innovation in those days. With his new tool he made six bales of cotton and picked all but a small portion of it himself.

As the years went by, Uncle Virgil became financially stronger, so he kept adding mules and cultivating more land until he had twelve mules and a horse under his care.

In 1940, Uncle Virgil bought his first tractor, a Ford. That was a day that I remember. There were not a lot of tractors around during that time. Farmers in our area just couldn't afford them and the war was on in Europe, so there weren't a lot of them being made. Having a tractor was a big deal!

During the 1940's was when Uncle Virgil had his biggest crops. Some years he would make two hundred bales of cotton. During his biggest years he would clear five or six thousand dollars at the end of the season.

Those were also the years Virgil bought most of his land. He owned about two thousand acres at one time, with eight tractors and numerous pieces of farm equipment.

During this time he saw a need for well digging as some prosperity returned after World War I. He developed a team of men to dig wells. The work was all done by hand shovels down to depths of perhaps 25 feet and about 3 feet wide. The well walls had to be perfectly straight or the wall might cave in on the digger. Dirt was removed from the well using a bucket and a windless, similar to drawing water from the well after it was finished.

For several years Uncle Virgil had one employee who did nothing but make concrete well curbs every day. These curbs would be let down in the completed well to prevent cave-ins. It was said that Uncle Virgil dug more wells and sold more well curbs than anyone else in Macon County during that period of time.

Uncle Virgil was diversified in his farming practices. He rotated his crops sometimes planting Crota Laria, Spectabilis, Lupine, Australian Peas, and field peas. These were all legumes that added nitrogen and humus making the soil productive and fertile. Uncle Virgil always used large quantities of commercial fertilizer. He worked long hard hours and always told me, "Hard work won't hurt anybody."

Back in 1907 Uncle Virgil had become a member of the Methodist Church and taught Sunday School from 1926 until a few years before his death.

In May of 1934 at the age of 37, Uncle Virgil married Nora Brooks. Nora died in 1949. Virgil married Jessie Johnson, the daughter of a Methodist Minister later that year.

Uncle Virgil and his wives did not have children of their own. Instead they took foster children, from one to several at a time. Some only stayed a short time, others stayed years. Uncle Virgil was elected in 1945 to the membership of the Macon County Commissioner's Court; a position he was reelected to for 20 years.

When Uncle Virgil died at age 84, I traveled home to celebrate his life here on earth. At his funeral a number of his foster children were present. They were well groomed, nicely dressed and some had come a great distance in order to be there.

I was fortunate to be, like his foster children, one of the young people Uncle Virgil had inspired and encouraged. What a legacy he left. And I know I will see him again.

# Traveling Rural Alabama

My mother, Carrie Lula White, was the daughter of John and Lula White. Grandma was originally from Griffin, Georgia but she and Grandpa John lived in Dadeville for most of my mother's youth.

Grandpa John was a Baptist Minister and was in different businesses over the years. He owned dry goods stores, department stores, a Pontiac dealership, and cotton gin. I guess it was 1937 when Grandpa John moved to Albertville, Alabama and purchased a dry goods store. He sold everything possible except fresh meat and produce.

The store was a success when Grandpa John took on another endeavor, he bought a cotton gin inside the city limits of Albertville, Alabama. I'll tell you about working in the cotton gin later on.

When I was young, Mother's parents lived in central Alabama, about 160 miles from our home. Making that trip isn't like it is today. Going to see my grandparents would take us all day and it was always quite an adventure.

The car my daddy was driving in those days was the same 1920's model held together with bailing wire that he hauled produce and chickens in. That car always had issues with reliability and on top of that, tires, even new ones, were not very good.

The roads we traveled were all dirt, or mud if it had been raining. The only time we would see a paved road might be a little swath through the center of a small town. The roads were so narrow two cars sometimes couldn't pass each other, so if another car was coming in the opposite direction, someone had to pull over and stop to let the other guy go by.

Pot holes littered the roads back then so it wasn't uncommon for tires to blow out. I remember lots of times seeing someone on the side of the road fixing a tire. There were a few times when we were one of those because daddy had a tire go flat. I guess that was why it was common practice to carry a tube repair kit, a jack, a tire pump, and at least two spare tires in the trunk or tied to the car.

This was the 1930's when the country just wasn't as populated. We would travel several miles between towns and even between houses in many areas. Of course, there were no rest stops and almost no public restrooms accessible to travelers along the roadways; our only choice sometimes was going on the side of the road.

Momma always carried food (usually fried chicken and biscuits or a sandwich) and water with us. It's not like today with restaurants all over the place, the best you might be able to do was a country store with cheese and crackers for sale.

I have a lot of memories of those trips and the time we spent with my grandparents. I can still almost taste Momma's fried chicken.

# Money in the Bank

From a very early age my parents insisted that I use correct English. The use of slang and illiteracy were prevalent in the community and my parents believed that speaking proper English and being able to read and write would ensure my future success.

My mother made sure I was able to read before I started school. We couldn't afford books, but I would borrow Little Big Books from a friend and anytime I could get my hands on a newspaper I would read the funnies. Dick Tracey, Ally Oop and Dagwood were some of my favorites.

My parents emphasized reading, writing, and English composition. Momma and Daddy always said they wanted me to go to college, so school work came first. Watching my parents and other family members work hard motivated me early to find a way to earn money.

Through the years I had different jobs and I met different people that helped me by offering me advice and work. At a young age I embarked on a lifetime of learning how different businesses operated, interacting with people of all walks and stations of life, and becoming a curious student in the observation of the character and behaviors of people.

In 1941 when we were living in Arab, Alabama, I was 14. There were no jobs for boys to make any kind of money. So I decided the best way for me to make money of my own was to farm. I talked to Daddy about what I wanted to do and he agreed to help me. Daddy had farmed growing up so he knew how things needed to be done, what I would need, and I would be depending a lot on his guidance. He must have really had faith in me because he borrowed $250 on a signature loan from the bank and rented me 29 acres at $5 per acre.

The deal was that I had to pay the $145 in rent, in full, when the crop came in. Once we had the land Dad started going to horse and mule auctions. At one auction he found and bought a nice female mule weighing about 900 pounds, I named her Jake. I know!

We had a barn on the property. Dad found a used one horse (or one mule for me) wagon with a Georgia stock, and a one horse (mule) turning plow. We had just enough money left to buy seed and fertilizer.

Every day after school and on Saturdays Jake and I plowed the land until 20 acres were done. Then I hired a boy from school whose dad had a tractor to do the last 9 acres.

One incident that happened while I was plowing the land taught me a real lesson. It's also an example of the great irony of me and the times. This happened when Jake and I were working a low place covering about an acre that was too wet to plow initially.

Now remember, I'm in the serious business of farming with a lot on the line, and oh yeah, I'm 14 years old.

This low spot was located about a half a mile from our house across a main highway. I hitched up Jake and we plowed two or three rounds. As I was ready to turn, in the furrow I saw a black snake that was about two or three feet long. My first thought was, "I wonder if my mule would like to see a snake." I picked up a stick and put it down to the snake so he could wrap himself around it. Then I put the snake up to the mule.

At first Jake didn't do anything, but before I knew it she put her nose up to the snake and back went her ears. That was never a good sign. Jake snorted and took off like a race horse out of the gate headed towards the house with the plow still hooked to her.

The plow hopped up and down off the ground as Jake headed towards the highway. I was afraid she was going to hurt herself and was running as fast as I could to catch up.

Momma was sitting on the porch shelling peas when she saw Jake tearing over the hill, plow still attached and me trailing her as fast as I could go. Jake ran across the main road right up to the gate of her pen and stopped.

Jake didn't get hurt and neither did I, well except my pride maybe. I had made a real dumb decision that almost cost me everything I had, my mule, my plow. It could have all turned out so different, what if Jake had been hit by a vehicle?

When Momma asked me later what had happened I told her about introducing Jake to a snake. She didn't think that was one of my smarter decisions and asked me if I understood how if I had made the decision to just leave that snake alone, my plowing would be done and I wouldn't have put my mule, my equipment and myself in danger. Boy, did I understand.

I learned my lesson that day and the moral of that story was every action does in fact create a reaction...oh and don't show a snake to your mule!

When it was time to plant, Daddy borrowed a mule and planter from a neighbor to help me and Jake put the crops in. We put in eleven acres of cotton and the rest was corn, sweet potatoes, Irish potatoes, and watermelon. I put the watermelon in the middle of my corn so people wouldn't see them and borrow them. A trick my Daddy taught me.

When school finally got out for the summer I was farming full time. In the fall it was time to pick the cotton and I needed help! I bought a scale to weigh cotton and hired folks from the community to pick cotton. I paid them by the pound of picked cotton. The money I got later for selling my cotton seed paid for the pickers.

Eight bales of cotton came out of those 11 acres and with England at war the price of cotton had doubled from the time I planted to the time I harvested.

That first year I had more sweet potatoes than we could eat and sell... way too many. The corn we ate and I sold some to grocery stores for 5 cents an ear. We had enough corn left to feed Jake for a year. When it was all said and done, I paid off the bank loan of $250 dad had taken out, paid my land rent, and put $500 in the bank.

The next year dad only rented 15 acres and I put eight of it into cotton and the rest corn. I made about the same amount of money as I had the year before, but I didn't have to pay off a loan and my land rent was lower.

In the fall of 1942, after I finished gathering the crops in Arab, we moved to Albertville. Dad and I decided to let the mule pull the wagon loaded with farm equipment and me for the more than 20 mile trip.

Jake and I left early one morning stopping from time to time for a rest and a drink of water. We rested at noon so Jake could have some corn before we started down the steep grade of Brindlee Mountain near Guntersville. A grown man probably wouldn't have looked forward to making that trip, let alone a 15-year-old kid.

I had replaced the two wheel brakes, but Jake did have to hold the wagon back for nearly a mile as the brakes weren't strong enough. Then Jake had to pull the loaded wagon up Sand Mountain. We did not reach Albertville until after dark.

That day Jake made me real proud, I depended on her to hold back and keep us from speeding down the hill and she did a great job. She was sure a good ole' mule and that day she definitely earned her keep because we made the trip with no trouble.

I never abused Jake and it was days like that which made me want to make sure she was taken care of. Even after I bought a tractor I kept Jake and made sure she had plenty of feed and shelter. It wasn't until after I left for the Army that dad sold Jake.

The third year of my farming career dad wanted to go in with me, so he rented 40 acres across the road from where we lived. Dad bought a mule he named Red because of its reddish colored coat. We shared the work and the expense to put 40 acres into cotton and corn.

At the end of the year I decided I wanted to buy a tractor, so I searched around to see if one was available. With the war on there weren't many new tractors around, but I got lucky when I found a farmer that was retiring with a nice little Farmall Offset he wanted to sell.

I bought the tractor, but it didn't turn out to be a good deal for me. We had some hilly areas on our land and the tractor was heavier on one side (hence the name offset) and it, would get off center on inclines and tended to turn over.

I had a couple of scary experiences and decided this wasn't the tractor for me. I contacted the man that I bought it from and told him what had happened. He was so excited to hear from me because he wished he had never sold that tractor and he wanted it back. He paid me what I had bought it for, so we were both happy.

I went back on the hunt and found a used Allis Chalmers tractor. It was better balanced and worked good for me, after I put a new crank shaft in it that is. I had that tractor for right up until I went into the Army. You know I sold it for the same amount I bought it for, plus I made money the year I used it. It was a good investment.

I mentioned before that Grandpa John owned a cotton gin and he was partners with my Uncle Hollis White. Whenever I wasn't going to school or farming I would help at the cotton gin.

Farmers brought their cotton to the gin where the lint was separated from the seed. If a farmer wanted to take his seed home it would go through a large suction to a bin to be stored and later dumped into his wagon or truck.

If the farmer wanted to sell the seed it would go through a different suction to a seed storage area. When the area was full of seed, it would be loaded into a truck to be transported to Birmingham to sell.

It was common practice to put up to six tons of seed in a one and a half ton truck. They were always overloaded. I guess I was about 16 or 17 when I started driving the overloaded trucks 65 miles to Birmingham.

Working in a cotton gin was dangerous. Most of the time I worked as half of a two man team on the hydraulic press that baled the cotton. One man could operate the press but it took two men to handle the

500 pound bales.

The press was a piece of machinery prone to sudden hydraulic leaks. If it let go while you had fingers or arms in the way it could be traumatic. Plus there were numerous large belts (some the width of your hand or wider) turning all the equipment necessary to gin cotton at a high rate of speed. The belts were often made of leather or canvas and when they snapped it was never a good situation.

My grandfather and uncle always warned me to never stand in front of or directly in line with a belt. I can still hear them say, "Stay away, as far away as you can."

We had to set the press with the bagging that would be wrapped around the bale and set the metal straps. Once the cotton was compressed and the bale was made and released, each of us would hook into it and sling it off the press. Each bale weighed 450 to 500 pounds so we learned how to handle a bale without lifting it off the floor. One thing I did with the money I made was finally go to a dentist. I had never been to a dentist, it was a luxury my family just couldn't afford. It was necessary for him to pull one tooth and fill several others. Throughout the years every dollar I earned my parents allowed me to keep. They never asked me to contribute to the family budget. Maybe I didn't realize it at the time, but my parents were teaching me some very important lessons, about commitment, work, and always making sure you have some money in the bank.

# My Family

My Family

Marilou and I were fortunate to have 5 healthy children:

| | | |
|---|---|---|
| Son: | Lane | |
| | Born 1953 | |
| Daughter: | Karen | |
| | Born 1957 | |
| Daughter: | Brenda | |
| | Born 1959 | |
| Son: | Forrest  (Kent) | |
| | Born 1961 | |
| Daughter: | Jill | |
| | Born 1962 | |

Lane and Karen were mentioned earlier in the book.  Brenda and Kent were born at the end of our time in Birmingham.  Jill was born after our move to Mobile.  We are very proud of them all!

*Forrest Guthrie*

# Conclusion

It's been an amazing journey. I could never have imagined the twists and turns my life would take. All the amazing things I would be privileged to see and participate in. To not just study history, but to actually walk in it, seeing the people and events and hearing the conversations.

This is a great country....one like the world has never seen before. I pray that it continues and provides the opportunities I had to anyone who grabs them.

I wish to thank all those who assisted me in writing this story. Marilou, Linda, and my son Lane who assisted greatly in its completion when others were overcome with life events. I hope you have enjoyed reading it as much as I enjoyed telling it. My writing may not be that of a top novelist, but everything I have related in the book happened as I have said.

Forrest Guthrie

# Links

We thought you may enjoy videos from trips mentioned in the book. Below are a few links to videos on YouTube. Please note, we do not maintain the site these videos are stored on nor do we have or a copyright to these videos. The links below take you to the video owners site on YouTube.

White Limo footage of Kennedy riding to the Armory for his Acceptance speech, SAIC Guthrie is driving the car:
http://www.youtube.com/watch?v=8DvBSM99eKQ

Jackie Kennedy's trip to India. SAIC Guthrie was part of the detail team on this trip. This video is part 1 of the trip.
http://www.youtube.com/watch?v=-c7BaTtZsi0

Jackie Kennedy's trip to India. SAIC Guthrie was part of the detail team on this trip. This video is part 2 of the trip. If you want to have a little extra fun with this video, pay close attention around the 1:40 marker and you will find SAIC Guthrie.
http://www.youtube.com/watch?v=t6y39Vn-3kA